Charles Augustus Vansittart Conybeare

The Place of Iceland in the History of European Institutions,

being the Lothian Prize Essay, 1877

Charles Augustus Vansittart Conybeare

The Place of Iceland in the History of European Institutions,
being the Lothian Prize Essay, 1877

ISBN/EAN: 9783337316235

Printed in Europe, USA, Canada, Australia, Japan

Cover: Foto ©ninafisch / pixelio.de

More available books at **www.hansebooks.com**

THE PLACE OF ICELAND IN

THE HISTORY OF

EUROPEAN INSTITUTIONS:

BEING THE

LOTHIAN PRIZE ESSAY, 1877.

BY

C. A. VANSITTART CONYBEARE, B.A.

LATE JUNIOR STUDENT OF CHRIST CHURCH, OXFORD;
AND ASSISTANT MASTER AT MANCHESTER GRAMMAR-SCHOOL.

" orð mer af orði
orðs leitaði,
verk mer af verki
verks leitaði."
Hávamál 141.

Oxford and London:
JAMES PARKER AND CO.
1877.

Χαῖρε, καὶ ἐν νεφέλαισι καὶ ἐν νιφάδεσσι βαρείαις
καὶ πυρὶ καὶ σεισμοῖς νῆσε σαλειομένη·
ἐνθάδε γὰρ βασιλῆυς ὑπερβιον ὕβριν ἀλίξας
 Δῆμος Ὑπερβορέων, κόσμου ἐπ' ἐσχατιῇ,
αὐτάρκη βίοτον θείων τ' ἐρεθίσματα Μοισῶν
 καὶ θεσμοῖς ἁγνῆς εὗρεν ἐλευθερίας.
                                        Robert Lowe.

TO

CONRAD MAURER

AND

GUÐBRANDR VÍGFUSSON.

CONTENTS.

	PAGE
ANALYSIS OF ESSAY	vi
CHRONOLOGICAL TABLE	ix
LIST OF AUTHORITIES	xi
ESSAY—Part I.	1
,, ,, II.	68
,, ,, III.	109
APPENDIX A.	143
,, B.	ib.
,, C.	144
,, D.	145
,, E.	146
,, F.	147

PREFATORY NOTE.

To any one writing on Iceland, the elaborate works of the learned Maurer afford at once a help and a difficulty,—a help, in so far as they shed the fullest light upon the subjects of which they treat; a difficulty, in that their painstaking completeness has brought together well-nigh everything that can be said. I have not, therefore, in the following pages thought it necessary to do more than add references to his writings, where it seemed necessary to do so. Mr. Carlyle has observed ("Early Kings of Norway," p. 2), that "next to nothing has been shewn in English histories (*Rapin's excepted*) of the many and strong threads of connexion between English affairs and Norse." After looking over the ponderous tomes of Rapin's History, I have failed to find that exhaustive treatment of the subject which Mr. Carlyle's words would lead one to expect.

I have thought it best to add in notes a good deal that served to illustrate the text, in addition to mere references to original authorities (which I have in all cases where possible consulted); and on a few important questions, which, though closely connected with the main subject, I could not conveniently introduce into the text, I have ventured to add longer notes in the form of Appendices.

I am greatly indebted to Mr. F. York Powell, of Ch. Ch., for his kindness in helping me to revise and prepare this essay for publication; as also to my colleague at Manchester, Mr. Joseph Hall, for his careful revision of the proof-sheets.

ANALYSIS.

PART I.—GROWTH OF THE COMMONWEALTH.

SECT.
1. Importance of Iceland, p. 1.
2. Interest attaching to Iceland for Englishmen, p. 2.
3. National characteristics of the Northmen, p. 4.
4. Icelandic Literature: its Historical value, p. 6.
5. Discovery of Iceland: age of the Vikings, p. 9.
6. Ancient Social Condition of Norway, p. 11.
7. No privileged ruling caste in the Teutonic system, p. 14.
8. Ancient Political organisation of Norway, p. 15.
9. Karl the Great's Imperial Policy extends to Scandinavia, p. 18.
10. Harold Fairhair subdues Norway, p. 20.
11. The Emigration to Iceland, p. 23.
12. Character and Duration of the Emigration, p. 24.
13. The Landnámtide: erection of Temples, p. 25.
14. Origin of the Goðorð system: nature of the Goðorð, p. 27.
15. The Goði, or Priest, p. 29.
16. Nature of his Office and Authority: extent of his Jurisdiction, p. 33.
17. The Lögmaðr, p. 34.
18. Comparison of Iceland with Norway, p. 35.
19. Ulfljót establishes the Althing, p. 37.
20. The Lögsögumaðr, or Speaker, p. 41.

SECT.
21. Political effects of Ulfljot's reform with reference to the authority of the Goðar, p. 43.
22. The Reforms of Thord Gellir, p. 44.
    (I.) Division of Iceland into Quarters and Things, p. 46.
    (II.) Reform of the Althing, p. 49.
23. The Meeting of the Parliament, p. 51.
24. Thord Gellir's Reforms considered with reference to their Political Results, p. 53.
25. Political Crisis: necessity of further Reforms, p. 56.
26. Njál proposes his Reform Bill, p. 58.
27. Analysis of his Reforms: the Fimtardómr, p. 60.
28. Erection of new Goðorðs: Political Consequences, p. 62.
29. Reform of the Lögrétta, p. 65.
30. Njál's intentions frustrated, p. 67.

PART II.—ICELANDIC LAW.

31. Importance of Icelandic Law, p. 68.
32. Idolatry for forms of Legal procedure, p. 69.
33. Principles on which Icelandic Law is based: duty of Revenge: System of Compensation: Weregild, p. 71. The Hólmgang, or Wager of Battle, p. 73.
34. The Búakviðr, or Inquest of Neighbours; based on the principle of Self-government, p. 73.
35. Private Courts of Justice, p. 76.
36. Murder and Manslaughter in Icelandic Law, p. 78.
37. Comparison with English Criminal Law, p. 79.
38. Capital Punishment in Iceland, p. 81.
39. Of Arbitration and Atonements, p. 81.
40. An Icelandic Law-suit: Preliminary Proceedings, p. 85.

SECT.

41. Importance of Oaths and of technical accuracy, p. 87.
42. The Pleading, p. 89.
43. The Defence, p. 93.
44. The Appeal in the Fimtardómr, p. 95.
45. Failure of the Suit, p. 97.
46. Origin of the Jury-system discussed, p. 99.
47. Comparison of Icelandic with Anglo-Saxon Courts, p. 104.
48. Nature of the Northern Influence in England, p. 106.

PART III.—INTRODUCTION OF CHRISTIANITY, AND FALL OF THE REPUBLIC.

49. General Sketch, p. 109.
50. Christianity introduced by Law, p. 111.
51. The Church advances towards the acquisition of Temporal Power, p. 113.
52. Questions of Supremacy, &c., lead to Disputes between Church and State, p. 115.
53. Defects of the Goðorð system, p. 118.
54. Internal disturbances and disorder, p. 121.
55. Union of Iceland with Norway, p. 122.
56. Criticism of the Icelandic Constitution, p. 125.
57. The Polity of Scandinavia different from that of the Southern Teutons: Parallel between Iceland and England, p. 127.
58. Feudalism in England, Norway and Iceland, p. 130.
59. Analysis of Feudalism, p. 133.
60. Elements of Feudalism in Iceland, p. 135.
61. Development of Feudalism in Iceland different from Continental Feudalism, p. 138.
62. Conclusion, p. 140.

CHRONOLOGICAL TABLE.

A.D.
871. Ingólfr discovers Iceland.
,, Danes invade Wessex: Ælfred King.
872. Harald Haarfagr sole ruler of Norway.
874. Danes conquer Mercia.
876. Danes settle in Northumbria.
878. Danes overrun Wessex: Peace of Wedmore.
890—900. Rush of Settlers from the British Isles to Iceland.
893. Danes in the Thames.
900—920. Third Period of the Landnámtide.
901. Death of King Ælfred.
912. Northmen settle in Normandy.
929. Ulfljót establishes the Althing.
930. Hrafn Ketilsson, Lögsögumaðr.
930—935. Njál born.
935. Hakon, Athelstan's foster-son, King of Norway.
950. Þórarinn Raga bróðer, Lögsögumaðr.
965. Thord Gellir's Reforms: Division of Iceland into Quarters.
970. Þorkell Þorsteinsson, Lögsögumaðr.
981. Bishop Frederic comes to Iceland: first tidings of Christianity.
982. Discovery of Greenland.
984. Bishop Frederic proclaims Christianity at the Althing.
985. Þorgeirr Ljosvetninga-goði, Lögsögumaðr.
986. Bishop Frederic leaves Iceland.

A.D.
994. Swegen invades England.
995—1000. Olaf Tryggvason, King of Norway.
996—997. Mission of Stefnir Thorgilsson to Iceland.
997. Arrival of Thangbrand in Iceland.
1000. Christianity established by Law in Iceland.
,, Death of Olaf Tryggvason.
1002. Grimr Svertingsson, Lögsögumaðr.
1004. Erection of the Fifth Court: Skapti þoroddsson, Lögsögumaðr.
1006. Abolition of the Holmgang.
1011. Burning of Njál.
1012. Great Law-suit between Mord and Flósi.
1013. All England submits to Swegen.
1017. Knut, King of England.
1024. Attempt of Norway to annex Iceland repudiated by the Icelanders.
1027. Birth of William of Normandy.
1031. Steinn þorgestzson, Lögsögumaðr.
1042. Eadward the Confessor.
1047—1066. Harald Harðráða, King of Norway.
1066. Battle of Senlac.
1080. Death of Bishop Isleifr.
1082. His son Gizur consecrated Bishop.
1085. Failure of Danish Invasion of England.
1097. Introduction of Tithes into Iceland.
1101. Skálholt made a Bishop's see.
1107. A second Bishopric established at Hólar.
1117. Icelandic Laws first written down.
1238. No Althing held on account of civil disturbances.
1262—1264. Union of Iceland with Norway.

LIST OF THE PRINCIPAL WORKS CONSULTED.

ENGLISH AUTHORS.

Stubbs, Constitutional History.
,, Charters Illustrative of English History.
Freeman, The Norman Conquest.
,, The English Constitution.
Palgrave's English Commonwealth.
Hallam's Middle Ages.
Lappenberg's Normans in England.
Sir H. Maine, Village Communities.
,, Early Institutions.
Sir J. F. Stephen's English Criminal Law.
Worsaae, Danes in England.
Dasent, Story of Burnt Njál.
,, Essay on Iceland; Oxford Essays, 1858.
Laing's Sea-Kings of Norway.
Sir E. Head's Translation of Viga Glum's Saga.
Thorpe's Translation of the Poetic Edda.
Paijkull, A Summer in Iceland; Barnard's Translation.
Robertson's Historical Essays.
Blackstone's Commentaries.

ICELANDIC AUTHORS, &c.

Vigfússon's Icelandic Dictionary.
Ari hinn Fróði, Islendingabók, ed. Th. Möbius.
Grágás, ed. Schlegel.

The Edda, ed. Lüning.
„   ed. Bugge.
Snorro Sturluson, Heimskringla ; ed. Unger.
Sagan af Njali Þorgeirsyni. Copenh., 1772.
Sagan af Gunnlaugi-Ormstungu, &c. ; ed. Hafn, 1775.
Jón Arngrimsson de Rebus Islandorum.

GERMAN AUTHORS.

Konrad Maurer's Island.
„   Die Entstehung der Islandischen Staats.
             Beiträge, vol. i.
Dahlmann's Forschungen, vol. i.

FRENCH AUTHORS.

Guizot, Civilisation en Europe.
Bounechose, Histoire d'Angleterre.
De Coulanges, Institutions, &c., de l'ancienne France.

LATIN AUTHORS.

Tacitus' Germania.
Cæsar's Comm. de Bello Gallico.

PART I.

GROWTH OF THE ICELANDIC COMMONWEALTH.

§ 1. ICELAND—its Inhabitants, its Institutions, its Literature—too long neglected, has at length won from the Historians of Europe that recognition, to which its importance fully entitles it. To the Student of History, and to the Political Philosopher, Iceland must ever be a source of profound interest: for it is in that land, in the history of its people and its institutions, as he reads it in their unexampled literature, that he finds the key to much that would otherwise remain obscure in the history of his own country, be he German or English. In the Iceland of the ninth and tenth centuries he finds himself at home, as it were, amongst a people who are his kinsmen, endowed with the same characteristics, the same feelings, the same language as himself. But above all, he finds in the political life and social institutions, in the legal forms and national customs of that noble race, germs of those very institutions with which he is himself most familiar, and of which he is most proud,—germs which, common to the whole Teutonic family, have, in the course of centuries, become modified by different conditions and varying influences, and developed into the diverse systems of the present day. The Constitution of England is in its origin and

Importance of Iceland.

growth almost entirely Teutonic [a], and owes next to nothing to the Roman occupation, which left behind it little more than a few relics to prove the skill of the Roman engineer. Hence, just as the history of ancient Greece and Rome is important, because it enables us to study in their simplest forms many of those political and social problems, which to-day, owing to their complexity, are difficult to comprehend; just as the philosopher turns to the primitive legal codes of India or of Ireland, to seek the true meaning of many a difficult, and seemingly inexplicable, custom which now prevails; so the student of English history will find in the records of his Scandinavian forefathers, much that serves to illustrate and interpret "that ancient collection of unwritten maxims and customs, which is called the common law;" and the student of Foreign history will learn much that solves, by way of contrast, the problems offered by Continental systems.

Interest attaching to Iceland for Englishmen.

§ 2. Especially interesting to an Englishman must that land be, which became the home of freedom at a time when all other nations were passing under the yoke of tyranny; whose inhabitants were fired with that same spirit of independence, and enthusiastic love of liberty, which has ever since been the most marked characteristic of their latest descendants. England—perhaps the only land in the universe, as

---

[a] Cp. Stubbs, Const. Hist., i. p. 6. "If its history is not the perfectly pure development of Germanic principles, it is the nearest existing approach to such a development ... England developed its own common law free from the absolutist tendencies of Roman jurisprudence." Cp. also pp. 10, 11.

Judge Blackstone did not hesitate to affirm, in which political or civil liberty is the very end and scope of the constitution—may well feel an affection for the sister isle, tossed in the billows of the Northern Ocean, whose brave sons first set the example of resistance to the oppressor. The Englishman of to-day traces in the wild career of the earlier Viking a foreshadowing of that dash and daring, which caused the very names of Drake and Raleigh, Hawkins and Cavendish, to strike terror into the foreign foe. Proud of the Arctic exploits of a Frobisher, a Parry, a Nares, he recognises in the earlier Icelander the first colonist of Greenland, and the discoverer of the New World, ages before Columbus sailed across the Atlantic[b]. That same impatience of despotism, which drove so many brave men and true from their homes in Norway in search of "free land," many ages later impelled our Puritan forefathers to leave their homes in England in quest of "free religion" in the far West. Historians have remarked that the English barons were ever the stoutest defenders of freedom against ambitious

[b] Greenland was discovered in 982. Cf. Islendingabók, c. 6. The origin of the name is curious. The first discoverer, we read, called it *Green*-land, in the hope that its attractive name might induce others to settle there. "Vineland," which is mentioned in the same chapter as being apparently well-known, is allowed to be America, and was probably "no other than some part of the North American continent near Rhode Island or Massachusetts," (Das. Burnt Nj. cxvi.) But Dahlmann thinks it was the country between the coast of Labrador and Hudson's Straits, which perhaps accords more with the question of time, by which the discovery is verified; cf. Vigf. Dict. s. v. *eykt*.

kings, and it is to their respect for the proper liberties of the people, that they still owe their quiet possession of power. It is truly remarkable, as one author writes, that the "love of bodily exercises, games, hunting, and horse-racing, not to mention the predilection for daring sea-voyages so strongly prevalent amongst Englishmen, was also manifested, according to the Sagas, by the rich and powerful in Iceland." Nor can it be doubted that it is to the seafaring instincts of the same race, that England owes that naval supremacy which has long been her glory, and is still her strength.

<small>National Characteristics of the Northmen.</small> § 3. From the earliest times the characteristics of the Teutonic race seem to have been the same. A fearless courage, and unflinching contempt for death. A fixed determination to achieve some feat, which will secure a lasting fame [c], before the fated hour of doom arrives, which nothing can avert,—

"For death with them is made the road to fame."

A proud independence of spirit, conscious that it was born to rule, not to be ruled, combined with an inborn sense of justice, a real horror of lying and treachery, and withal a tenderness and gentleness of character in many an old heathen, worthy of the best of Christians: such is the fair side of their character. It has, it is true, a darker side

---

[c] Cp. Hávamál, 75:—

Deyr fé, deyja frœndr,
Deyr sjálfr it sama;
En orðstirr deyr aldregi
Hveim er ser góðan getr.

as well. The lawless ferocity of the Vikings in their world-wide depredations, which caused their name to be a terror to all nations, and a byword of cruelty to later ages, is no unfounded calumny; and many a saying and legend in England itself still testify to the agonies they inflicted upon the country [d].

Perhaps the very earliest indication we find in Roman literature as to the character of the "hardy Norseman," is that which Cæsar gives in a speech of Ariovistus, Dux Germanorum. It is a mere touch; but so true to nature, as to stamp the speech at once as genuine. Ariovistus, in reply to proposals made by Cæsar, hurls this bold and proud defiance at the Roman general: "Cum vellet congrederetur, intellecturum quid invicti Germani, exercitatissimi in armis, *qui inter annos xiv. tectum non subissent*, virtute possent [e]." These words are quite in the spirit of many an instance that might be quoted from the Sagas. But the special point to notice is, the boast of not having been under a roof for fourteen years, a boast which may be compared with Snorro's estimate of the Viking [f]: "I thought he might well be called a sea-king, who never slept beneath sooty rafters, and never drank at the chimney-corner;" or the description in the Orkney Saga of how a Viking "for three winters

[d] Cp. Robertson's Essays, p. viii. The Dane still retains his place as the typical "enemy" in popular tradition.

[e] Cæsar, *de Bell. Gall.*, i. 36.

[f] Snor. Sturl. Heimskr., p. 28 [ed. Unger], Ynglinga Saga, c. 34. Half's Saga.

lay out in his ship of war, so that he never came under a sooty rafter."

Tacitus' description of the primitive Germans, who "gaudent muneribus, sed nec data imputant, nec acceptis obligantur," holds good of the subjects of King Olaf, who refuse to pay him tribute, but are willing enough to make him handsome presents. At the same time, it is only partly true. The Icelander would not indeed receive a gift in any way that tended to place him in an inferior position, even from a relative. But a departing friend or visitor had to be dismissed with a gift [kynnisgjöf]; and such gifts were obligatory, being a sign of good-will on the part of giver and of recipient. Again, there is a true ring about the answer given by Erlingr to King Olaf for his offer of an earl's title and a rich kingdom to boot: "*Hersar* were my forefathers, and I no better name will bear than they. But, sire, I would gladly be made by you greatest among those who bear that title [g]."

Icelandic Literature. Its historical value.

§ 4. And the Literature, from which so much of general and of historical interest is to be learnt, is in its way unparalleled. It is surely no small thing that, in an age when, in central Europe, learning scarcely extended beyond the monastery's walls, there should be flourishing in a small island, almost within the Arctic circle, a national literature in the highest sense of the term, unrivalled for richness and poetry; springing from "a general

[g] Fornmanna S. i. 299.

enthusiasm, which neither the extreme severity of the climate, nor the barrenness of the soil, nor the poverty of the Icelanders themselves, could quell[h]," there flourished between the tenth and the twelfth centuries a mass of literature which is all the more surprising, when it is recollected that no extant Saga was committed to writing before the fourteenth century[i]. Amongst the various causes to which such a body of strictly national literature owes its existence, is no doubt to be reckoned the national character, which their semi-secular position gave to the Icelandic clergy, who devoted themselves to founding an indigenous literature[k]. But chiefly it is due to the impulse given by the desire of learning and spreading news from abroad, whenever a strange vessel touched their shores; of hearing how their countrymen had acquitted themselves in foreign lands; and whether their island home was regarded by men of other nations with friendly or hostile feelings[l]. An amusing account is given in one Saga of the excitement which the return of Bishop Magnus from abroad occasioned; the Althing was being held, and public business was in full swing; but as soon as the news was received, the whole body of citizens arose, and neglecting their law-suits, hurried to meet him, and learn the latest news from Norway. The Scalds, too,

---

[h] So Lappenberg speaks of this "phenomenon which will never appear again." ("Normans in England," ed. Thorpe, p. 59.)
[i] Laing, "Sea-kings," i. 23. [k] Cf. Maurer, Isl., 95.
[l] Cp. Gunnlaugs S., ed. Hafn. 1775, p. 25.

were not merely poets. In an age when writing was still unknown [m], amongst a people who, being *udal*-born to land at home, were constantly taking part in predatory expeditions to foreign lands, they were a necessary institution, acting as the historians and biographers of later times. Hence it is that, after the fall of the Republic, the literature of the country sadly declined. Iceland truly deserves the title of the Athens of the North; the love of law, and the litigious spirit of its inhabitants, remind us of the ancient Athenians, even more than the splendour of their literature.

Of the Sagas it is needless to speak at any length. Many are historical biographies of the Kings of Norway, of which an estimate may best be formed from the following words of Mr. Dasent [n]: "Such sagas as these, written at various periods, by scribes more or less fitted for the task they had undertaken, are evidently of very varying authority; the most authentic of them being no doubt the Saga of Swerrir, King of Norway, who flourished at the end of the twelfth century. In its way it is equal to Thucydides, and of it it may be said, that the king was lucky in finding such an historian, and the writer in finding such a king to chronicle [o]."

---

[m] The runic characters do not appear to have been used for general purposes.   [n] Vigf. Dict., Introd., p. 46.

[o] The following classification of the chief branches of Icelandic literature is borrowed from Mr. Vigfusson:—

A. *Poetry*, (on which the Sagas are mostly based), Mythical,

Others, as the Njala, describing the home life of the Icelanders, and their adventures abroad, are "the most interesting, because the most truthful of all;" and hence, perhaps, the most valuable to the historian. The Islendingabók, which is merely an epitome of a far larger historical work, now lost, is a valuable guide to many points of Icelandic history. The Landnáma-bók, to which the above now forms a sort of introduction, is the "Domesday Book" of Iceland, and no less invaluable to the historian of that country. Further, the Icelanders were a most law-loving race, and no country of that date perhaps possesses such a vast treasure of ancient statutes, as we find, e.g. in the Grágás, or Icelandic Codes [p], and the Norges Gamle Love, or Old Laws of Norway.

§ 5. The discovery of Iceland by the Northmen took place towards the end of the ninth century; but it was some years before any attempt was made at settlement. The immediate cause of the emigration which streamed towards the island from Norway and the British Isles, between the years

Discovery of Iceland. Age of the Vikings.

Heroical, and Historical, e.g. Poetical Edda, Erik's Lay, Hornklofi's verses.

  B. *Laws* (of Iceland), Grágás; (of Norway), Norges gamle Love.
  C. *Mythical Histories*, e.g. Snorro's Edda, Volsung Saga.
  D. *Icelandic Sagas*, or Histories referring to Icelandic history.
    1. Sagas of the General History, e.g. Landnámabók.
    2. Sagas of Men or Families, e.g. Njúla.
    3. Sagas of Bishops,—Annals, &c.
  E. *Kings' Sagas*, or Lives of Princes of Foreign Countries, e.g. Heimskringla, the Orkney Saga, &c.

[p] Cf. App. A.

880 and 920, was the discontent engendered in the home country by the attempt of Haraldr Hárfagr to establish a feudal monarchy. The revolution brought about by his oppressive policy, seems to have thrown Norway into a convulsion, moral and social as well as political, which was shared by Sweden and Denmark, where like events had already taken place. The evidence of other countries, Irish, Welsh, Anglo-Saxon, and Frank, testifies to the external action of the vast forces which were thus brought into play; for the conquest of Normandy, and the Danish invasions of England, are the outcome of this period, as much as the settlement of Iceland. The existence of the Vikings, the fact that a large class of warriors, for the most part sons of kings and princes, had taken to piracy as a mode of living, could not but exercise a deep influence on all ranks of the population. And this influence tended to produce a general feeling of discontent, of impatience at old customs and settled forms. In religion, too, a like change becomes visible; the repeated contact into which the Viking expeditions brought large masses of the nation, the forms of other civilisations which thus became familiar to them, and the new ideas which they necessarily imbibed, all tended to bring about a scepticism and disbelief of the old forms of religion, which spread the more rapidly, inasmuch as there were no religious books to stereotype the old mythological beliefs, existing by tradition only; and no separate class of priests, whose business it was to foster a

state religion; for in the words of Dr. Maurer, "Keine Priesterkaste schob sich bei ihnen zwischen das Volk und seine Götter in der Mitte, keine Geheimlehre schied eine wissende Classe von einer nicht wissenden q."

§ 6. What then this old order of things was, which, it would seem, was so soon about to disappear in the presence of a higher and advancing civilisation, it will not be out of place to inquire, before following the emigrants to their new home in Iceland; for we shall find, when we come to examine the Constitution of the Icelandic Commonwealth, that much of their system, as indeed was only natural, was borrowed by the emigrants from their old home. Besides, when the necessity came for establishing a fixed form of government, Ulfljót, their first great lawgiver, spent three years in Norway, studying the old forms and customs, with the view of introducing them into Iceland. Therefore, a correct notion of the social and political condition of Norway before and at the time of the migration, will contribute to an accurate estimate of the form of government which grew up in Iceland. And first, as to the social condition of Norway.

Ancient Social Condition of Norway.

The population of every country in those early times was divided into serfs and freemen; and Scandinavia formed no exception to the general rule. Whence this distinction first arose in Norway, it is idle to ask: the fact that it was so must form our starting-point. That its origin was

q Isl., p. 21.

shrouded in the mists of antiquity, appears from the curious mythical account of the origin of the three classes—Thralls, Carls, and Jarls, which is preserved in the Rígsmál. There the Thrall is described in the following disparaging manner [r]:—

> "Edda a child brought forth, they with water
> Sprinkled its swarthy skin, and named it *Thrall*.
> It grew up, and well it throve; of its hands
> The skin was shrivelled, the knuckles knotty,
> And the fingers thick: a hideous face it had,
> A curved back and protruding heels.
> He then began his strength to prove,
> Bast to bind, make of it loads;
> Then faggots carried home, the livelong day."

Then Thrall took to himself a wife, and the Edda goes on to describe how this couple, from whom sprang the race of Thralls, "erected fences, fields manured, tended swine, kept goats, dug turf."

The lot of the Carl is a trifle better; we are not told much as to the child's personal appearance, save that "its eyes twinkled;" but its mother " in linen swathed the ruddy head," and when it grew up, it—

> "Learnt to tame oxen, make a plough, houses build,
> And barns construct, make carts, and the plough drive."

Thus we see that, so far as his occupation went, there is not so very much difference between him and the Thrall; but practically, as compared with

---

[r] Thorpe's translation is given, which, as he himself observes, is not elegant, though it is sufficiently literal.

the serf, he was, as Mr. Freeman says, "a privileged person. He is the simple freeman, the mere unit in the army or assembly, whom no distinction of birth or office marks out from his fellows." The true distinction, however, which raised him above the class below, and which is sufficiently marked in the above quotations, is that he owned land, which in those days was everything; whereas the Thrall was no better than a hired labourer.

Next, and highest in the social scale, comes the Jarl, or Earl. On his noble parentage, the graces of his person, his prowess and high-born spirit, the poet dwells with evident partiality, and at some length. So simple and picturesque is the following description, that no apology is made for quoting several verses. Of his parents we are told how—

"The husband sat, and twisted string, bent his bow,
And arrow shafts prepared: but the housewife
Looked on her arms, smoothed her veil,
And her sleeves fastened; her headgear adjusted.
A clasp was on her breast; ample her robe;
Her sark was blue, brighter was her brow,
Her breast fairer, her neck whiter than driven snow."

This is followed by a charming picture of the spreading of the banquet, which one omits with regret. Then, when the housewife brought forth a boy,—

"In silk they wrapt him, with water sprinkled him,
And named him Jarl.
Light was his hair, bright his cheeks,
His eyes piercing as a young serpent's.

> There at home Jarl grew up,
> Learnt the shield to shake, to fix the string,
> The bow to bend, arrows to shaft,
> Javelins to hurl, spears to brandish,
> Horses to ride, dogs to let slip,
> Swords to draw, swimming to practise."

Then Rîg teaches him runes, gives him his name, and bids him possess his own oðal-lands, and ancient dwellings; while his nobles come to a hall where dwelt Hersir (chief of a Herað), and,

> "There they found a slender maiden,
> Fair and elegant, Erna her name.
> They demanded her, and conveyed her home,
> So Jarl espoused her."

No privileged Ruling Caste in the Teutonic System. § 7. If we ask what was the definite position, and what the special privileges enjoyed by the Jarls, it is difficult to answer. No specific privileges appear to have been secured to this class by definite laws; but a comparison with the ruling class of other countries suggests the true relations between them and the Carls. "If we compare," writes Mr. Freeman, "the Swiss democratic cantons, we find that certain families, enjoying no legal privileges above their fellows, were held in a kind of hereditary reverence, and that members of those families were preferred above all others to the highest posts in the State." So, too, in England, old-established county families hold, in the eyes of their neighbours, a kind of privileged position, guaranteed not by the law, but by their own services to their own country, and the respect due to them in consequence. Nor can it be doubted that it is to the persistency throughout English history of Scandinavian feeling, that we owe the peculiarity of English society, and the absence of that curse of nations, a privileged ruling *caste* [s].

Setting apart, then, the Thralls, the whole social organisation of the ancient Scandinavian communities rests upon the possession of land. The great mass of the population consisted of the oðals-men, or Böndar. The type still survives in the statesmen of Westmoreland and Cumberland, whose pride of birth and ancestry is well known. All who possessed no land in Norway were Thralls. The oðal, or allodium (which is only the Latinized form of the old Norse word [t]), was a patrimony, and in a sense inalienable. It was the dearest possession of the independent Norseman; and, sooner than relinquish his right to the free ownership of the land of his fathers, and submit to the new-fangled land-scátt, or tax, which the monarch sought to impose, he was ready to leave his fatherland in search of a new home.

§ 8. Let us now turn to the political organisation, which had grown up on this ancient social classification. Before the time of Haraldr Hárfagr (i.e. till near the end of the ninth century), the political *Ancient Political Organisation of Norway.*

---

[s] Cp. Palgr. Engl. Comm., 33; May, Const. Hist., i. 285.

[t] Mr. Vigfusson suggests a new derivation of this word. In the old Norse, he says, there is a compound, *alda-oðal*, meaning a property of ages, or held for ages = *fundus avitus*. Hence the Latin, *all-odium* = property held in absolute possession, as opposed to that held in fee. (Cf. Dict. Addenda, s. v. oðal, p. 777.)

condition of Norway appears to have been very similar to that of the Teutonic tribes, described by Tacitus. The whole nation was broken up into numerous small shires or separate states (*fylki* = our folk), each ruled by its independent *fylkir*. These again were subdivided into districts called *heraðs*, with each its *hersir*, or chief. At the head of the whole nation, a chieftain seems to have been recognised as over-king: but it may be doubted whether he enjoyed any real supremacy, at least in the early times, over his brother kings. The titles of fylkir and hersir have reference especially to the warrior side of the chieftain's character, which however was not the only, nor hardly perhaps the most important, aspect in which he is to be regarded. The position of these independent chieftains was from the earliest times politico-religious[u]. Both the direction of the religious services belonging to the Temple, and the administration of public affairs, lay in their hands. The antiquity of this politico-religious organisation is shewn by the fact, that it is attributed to Odin in the Heimskringla; where the land is represented as divided into a number of districts large and small, each with its own property and temple, endowed with a poll-tax levied on the community. Each has its own Thing, or public assembly, held in or near the temple; each such district is presided over by a ruler, be he called Drottinn or Ko-

---

[u] Cf. Heimskr., p. 5, ed. Unger.

nungr[x], Hersir or Fylkir, who conducts all the temple services, administers justice, maintains peace throughout the district, and presides at all public meetings, for whatever purpose held. Such is the picture of the organisation represented to have been introduced by Odin. The legend about the God is manifestly unhistorical; but Snorro was evidently trying to account for a system with which he was acquainted, and which really existed; and the truth of his description is confirmed by its similarity to that state of things which we know to have existed in later times. For example, the organisation of the Church, after the introduction of Christianity, was clearly based upon this system. The different churches—some chief churches (höfuð-kirkjur), some district churches (heraðskirkjur), others again merely a sort of chapels-of-ease (hægindiskirkjur)—answer to the old heathen divisions of the country, and were more probably adopted from the primitive organisation, than introduced along with the new faith. Just as the old heathen custom, which required the chief to open a sitting of the þing, was at first practised by the Christian priest, but afterwards transferred to a special lay-officer. In the same way we shall, later on, find the churches in Iceland springing up in exactly the same manner that the old heathen temples, which they were superseding, had done.

Self-dependent as were the chieftains of these

[x] In the Rígsmál we find traces of the development of the King from the Jarl, for *Kon*, i.e. King, is the son of *Jarl*.

small kingdoms, the number of the latter contributed powerfully to the independence of the people; for the smaller the territorial subdivisions, the greater was the individual freeman's power and importance. The oðal-holders were wont to meet together in their heraðs, and fylkis-þings, and deliberate on matters of public interest; with them rested the final decision on all important political questions. The chiefs, or kinglets, were powerless before the unanimous will of the people, who by no means regarded them with that awe which the later fiction of the Divine Right of Kings is wont to inspire. Nor was the chief, any more than the poorest *bondi* exempted from the law of the land. No man, so ran the old Norse law, shall commit an assault on another, be he king or churl [r].

Karl the Great's Imperial policy extends to Scandinavia.

§ 9. Such was the social and political condition of Scandinavia till the second half of the ninth century. Then came a change which convulsed the North, and worked a revolution in the ancient order of things, not in Norway only, but throughout Scandinavia. It was an age of transition for all Western Europe. The movement begun by Karl the Great in the early part of the century was taking its course; and in England, in Denmark, and in Sweden, the same phenomena were visible. For just as Karl had aimed at establishing a strong empire in Central Europe, so, in the course of the ninth century, the West-Saxon Eg-

---

[r] Frostathingslag, iv. 50.

bert, in England, was securing the supremacy of the whole island[z]; so in Denmark, Gorm was establishing a monarchy; so in Sweden, Eirik Eymundsson, King of Uppsala, was strengthening the tottering "over-kingship," which then existed, into a regular sovereignty. In Norway, this consolidation of small independent states into a strong monarchy was carried out by Harald Hárfagr. He subdued one after another the petty Kings of Norway, and made himself, not till after many a hard struggle, sole ruler of the whole country. Those of the petty chiefs who submitted became the King's liegemen, the Jarls, being in dignity next after the King, answering to the Latin *Comes*, or German *Graf* [a]. In order to provide the revenues he required for the numerous benefices and fiefs, which he gave to his *Lendirmenn*, or liegemen, he subdued and imposed a land-tax upon the former freeholders. Hence the gradual degradation of old names, once titles of highest respect; the old *hersir* gradually became liegeman, and ranked below the Jarl, but above the *höldr* (or yeoman); while the time-honoured *bóndi* fell to the bottom of the scale, and like the English *boor* came to mean only the common, low people, as opposed to the King and his men (*hirð*).

[z] On the relation of this Anglo-Saxon policy to the Frank system, cp. Stubbs' Const. Hist., i. pp. 203, 204.

[a] It is curious that the title *Jarl* (earl) has become naturalised in England; but in the north (from whence it came) it has been completely superseded by *Graf*.

§ 10. To understand fully the meaning of this new policy, and to realise in its full extent the universal indignation which it excited,—an indignation so great and so general as to cause a wholesale emigration from the country,—it is necessary to enter a little more into the details of Norse land tenure at this period. Four sorts of tenure are distinguishable. (1.) There was the land originally occupied by each individual, by selection, while the right of ownership was as yet free to any one; or it may be, apportioned to each by a formal division of land. This was the oðal. It was inalienable, so that even when parted with, the possessor still retained a title (landsbrigð, *jus retrahendi*). (2.) There were certain lands which had never been distributed in severalty, which remained in possession of the community under the title of almenning (= *ager compascuus*). (3.) Tracts of such common land were often let out on lease [b], (even, as it seems, as a patrimony, which could be inherited,) the community being landlord. (4.) Lastly, one private individual could let land on lease to another, which was then called *leiguland*.

Marginal note: Harold Fairhair subdues Norway.

Now what King Harold appears to have done was this. In the first place, he appropriated to himself, as lord of the soil [c], all the lands which

---

[b] No distinct name is found for this tenure in Norway, but in Sweden it was called *almenningsjorð*.

[c] Cf. Heimskr., p. 51, (ed. Unger), which gives the details of the subdivision of districts, and describes how "each of the Jarls now had greater power and income than the kings had before en-

had formerly belonged to the communities; and all those who had hitherto paid any rent-charge to the community must thenceforth become tenants of the king. He also levied a poll-tax (*nefgildi*), which, however, was no innovation. In all this no revolutionary reform was involved; and had he gone no further, we should not perhaps find in the Sagas of that period such bitter complaints of the tyrant's oppression. But when the king further proceeded to levy a landskátt on those oðal-menn, or free land proprietors, who from time immemorial had lived on their own estates free from all impost, then indeed there arose an universal cry of indignation, which it is not difficult to sympathise with. Not only was an invasion thus attempted of the most cherished, nay, sacred rights of all who were free born throughout the land; but it swept away the only distinction which raised the allodial lords above those who were tenants either to the State or to private freeholders. For, in these early times, it was the *free* possession of land that conferred social and political distinction; and the loss of such property necessarily entailed loss of condition. Long after our present social system had grown up, did the same idea linger in the minds of the old landed gentry of England.

joyed," so that many great men joined the king and became his men. Harold's policy was not destined to be a permanent success, for Hakon the Good gave back to his subjects their rights, (Sag. Hak. God., c. 1,) and the ancient oðal institution remains to-day nearly the same as of old. Cf. also Orkneyinga S.

> "Alas! alas! 'tis all trouble hath left me,
> To cherishe me and my poor sister's life,
> If this were sold, our names should then be quite
> Rased from the bederoll of gentility [d]."

Much more keenly, then, must the proud Norsemen have felt the threatened degradation, and rather than submit to such an infringement of their rights, they resolved to seek a new home across the seas, and found a free country beyond the reach of the oppressor's arm. Many roved far and wide, harrying every coast from the Baltic to the Black Sea [e]; numbers settled at different points along the coasts of the British Isles; but it was to the newly-discovered Iceland that most of the exiled chiefs found their way, and soon the stream of emigration became so formidable, that King Harold, fearing that his realm would be left desolate, imposed a tax on all who should wish to leave the country [f]. It was, indeed, a migration *en masse*, and that, too, not of the meanest portion of the population; but on the contrary, the noblest and worthiest of the land, the most peaceably disposed, and the most cultivated, formed the great bulk of the emigrant host. While the most warlike of the nation sailed south-

---

[d] Heywood's "A woman killed with kindness," quoted by Kemble, "Anglo-Saxons," i. 88. Mr. Dasent remarks on the blessings conferred in the long run by Harold's policy, which, however, to the freeman of that day "was a curse." Burnt. Njál, i. p. ix.

[e] In the seventeenth century, the Algerians revenged themselves by harrying the Westmannafirth Isles.

[f] Cf. Islendingabók, c. 1.

wards and founded a new kingdom in Gaul, the richest landowners eventually settled in Iceland; which fact, coupled with the necessity imposed upon them of trading with the British Isles for the supply of many of their wants, accounts for the peaceable and even mercantile spirit which characterised the Icelanders.

§ 11. But the column of settlers by no means included only heathen chiefs from Norway. Norwegians, of course, formed the majority of the immigrants. But there was not wanting a fair sprinkling of Swedes and Goths, though apparently "not a single Dane g." An infusion of the Keltic nationality is testified by the names of Keltic origin, which occur in the Landnámabók; and here and there might be found an Anglo-Saxon in the Northman's family. Again, many were Norse chiefs, who had lived long years in foreign lands, and who were therefore imbued with foreign ideas. In religion, too, there was nearly as great diversity as in race. The majority, no doubt, were heathens sunk in superstition, men who worshipped rocks and waterfalls. Others, void of belief, and confident in their own might, refused to acknowledge any God. And, on the other hand, there was a handful of Christians who, on the preaching of the new faith in Iceland by Thangbrand, formed a nucleus, round which the converts were able to rally. Njál himself appears to have been a Christian at the time when the first tidings of Christianity reached the

The Emigration to Iceland.

g Cf. Maurer, Isl., p. 27.

island, for he at once declared himself in favour of the new faith, and "went often alone away from other men, and muttered to himself[h]."

Character and duration of the emigration.

§ 12. Although we have spoken of this great event as an emigration *en masse*, we do not mean that the colonists went forth as an organised body, under the command of a single chief, and carrying with them a fixed form of government, or a political organisation ready to be set up in their new home. So far from such being the case, they appear to have struggled across in the most haphazard way; many not even coming straight across, but halting for a time on the Faroe or Orkney isles, till the violence of Harold hunted them out, and compelled them to wander yet further, to escape the conqueror's wrath. In most cases, a family or a chief with his following would arrive together, or a few members of a family, out of which the remainder had preferred to submit to the conqueror's sway. Besides which, "sixty years," we read[i], "elapsed before the whole island was fully occupied, so that no more came after that." The land which was thus taken into possession was practically unoccupied; for the few Irish missionaries who had established a station on the island quickly left, and appear to have exercised absolutely no influence on the new-comers[k].

[h] Njála, c. lxiii.; Das., ii. 63.   [i] Islendingabók, c. 3.

[k] Cp. Islend., c. 3: "þá vóro her menn cristnir þeir es Norðmenn calla papa, en þeir fóro siðan á braut, af því at þeir vildo eigi vesa her við heiðna menn, ok léto eptir bökr irscar ok bjöllor ok bagla, &c." This last sentence seems to imply that they left in a hurry, and probably from fear.

§ 13. The newly-arrived settlers did not immediately set about establishing any form of government, and what local organisation arose in the course of time, sprang up spontaneously, as was to be expected from the straggling manner in which the emigrants had arrived, and the haphazard way in which they severally settled their future abodes[1]. The importance of this fact will appear presently, when we come to consider the real character of the *Goðorð*, around which centres the whole political organisation of the nation.

The Landnámtíde. Erection of Temples.

Each chief and band of immigrants, as they arrived, settled upon the spot they fixed upon, and at first very large tracts of indefinite extent were thus occupied by individual proprietors. But the inconvenience of this licence soon becoming felt, a limit was put upon the area to be occupied by each man or woman, apparently by King Harold's advice[m]. Yet the question still remains, how those managed, who came after all the available land had been taken into possession. Some few received it as a gift; though such cases were rare, even between kinsmen; for here the old national pride came in,

---

[1] For a description of the superstitious ceremonies connected with the selection and hallowing of the new dwelling-place, cf. Maur. Beitr., p. 45, sqq. The Christians seem to have adopted much the same plan as the heathens, Ib., 48, 49. "Bemerkenswerth ist übrigens, dass auch die Christlichen Ansiedler, welche sich, freilich nur in geringer Zahl von Anfang an in Island finden, *in ganz änlicher Weise* bei der Wahl ihrer Wohnung sich benehmen."

[m] Cf. Landnám, v. i. p. 214. The late settlers thought that those who had preceded them had taken too much land: "Then King Harold brought them to resolve that no man, &c."

which made it derogatory in the freeman to accept gifts without a return. Some even drove out the rightful owners, and seized their lands by violence. But, for the most part, such late arrivals were probably accommodated by purchasing land, or acquiring it by other forms, which it is not necessary to enquire into more particularly in this place, inasmuch as no important political effects immediately resulted therefrom. It is more to the present purpose to trace the way in which temples were erected, and became the nucleus around which the future communities gradually grew up.

That the number of these temples was very considerable, is proved by the frequency with which the word Hof occurs in local names. Every chief of note probably, who had the means, erected his own *hof* on his land, along with his *skáli* or mansion. From the very first a certain "congregation" would attend such a temple, in the persons of the family retainers and servants of the founder, who would in most cases be hofgoði or priest, as well as höfþingi or chieftain. In addition to these, there would be an attendance of all the neighbouring landowners, who from want of means had been unable to set up their own temple. And later arrivals, who obtained land in whatever way, on the *landnám* of hofgoði, would also as a rule become one of his congregation. Again, a chieftain with very extensive lands might build a number of temples: Geirmund, we are told, built four. In this case, though he might keep the priesthood of one of the number for himself, he would place dependants of his own in charge of the rest. And this fact suggests a remark as to the curious position held by these heathen priests. If a priest were also chief, his position was of course assured, but often we find slaves and freedmen set over temples. Thus in Landnáma, xi. 29. "Geirmund says: 'For this thine undertaking shalt thou receive thy freedom, and possess the temple of which thou wast in charge.' And from that day Atli was a man of note." The fact that a slave could administer the temple services, seems to indicate that but small consideration was in those days bestowed upon religious ceremonial. The slave, however, was put over the temple (at varðveita hofit) as the representative of his master; the old idea being that the slave was his master's property, and therefore, as it were, part of him. Hence his officiating in the temple was tantamount to his master's being there. From the instance quoted above, it is clear that it was the *possession* of a temple which conferred honour and dignity, probably owing to the income arising out of the temple dues (hoftollr).

§ 14. It was in this way, and around the temples thus erected, that the Goðorð or temple community gradually sprang up. It did not owe its origin to the relations immediately involved in the landnám, and the giving away or letting of land to other settlers. The political organisation of Iceland had its origin in the temple system, and not in any form of land tenure. The Goðorð was no doubt intimately con-

Origin of the Goðorð system. Nature of the Goðorð.

nected with the landnám of the most powerful of the immigrants; for it was they, for the most part, who having the means, built temples, round which when erected there gathered a community, composed no doubt chiefly of his own friends and adherents. But that there was *no necessary* connexion between the rights of the first settler over those who afterwards occupied allotments on his territory, and the formation of Goðorð is proved by the following facts, of which repeated instances are found in the Sagas. (1.) There were plenty of small, independent settlers, who betook themselves as þingmenn (or liegemen) to the temple of a neighbouring superior chief, without founding a Goðorð of their own. (2.) Goðorðs are not unfrequently found set up by persons settled on a stranger's landnám. (3.) The power of a Goði is often extended beyond his Goðorð to others, who were never settled on any landnáma belonging to him.

These considerations seem to imply that a Goðorð was the private property of its founder; and such it always was. Hence, a Goðorð could be alienated, bought, sold, given away, or bequeathed. If the proprietor of a Goðorð was going abroad, he could dispose of it for the term of his absence, and resume it on his return. And so, too, a Goðorð might pass into the hands of several partners, become, in fact, a sort of joint-stock company; in which case, it seems that the partners shared the þingmenn and the expenses, and took the religious duties in turn year by year. But as time went on, there was added to this purely private character of the Goðorð a public aspect as well. The "parishioners" (if we may use the term) who for a long time had been in the habit of attending the services of a particular temple, would also have something to say in the event of a change of ownership. This aspect of the Goðorð, as implying a public function, is recognised in the provision made for the proper performance of the duties by deputy, in the event of the Goðorð falling by inheritance into the hands of a minor or of a woman; or when the Goði himself is ill, or lives too far off. So, too, in later times at least, penalties are inflicted for nonfulfilment of duty on the Goði; and in extreme cases, the Goðorð may be sequestrated, in which case "the þingmenn shall parcel out the Goðorð among themselves[n]." Lastly, in the event of its changing hands, the þingmenn seem always to have had it in their power to resist the intrusion of a new Goði, to whom they entertained any strong objection.

§ 15. The nature of the circumstances under which the settlement took place, points to the conclusion that the immigrants brought with them, and sought to reproduce in their own home, as much of the old organisation with which they had been familiar in the home country, as the new conditions in which they found themselves placed would allow. To see how far this was really the case, it is necessary to consider in some detail the new Goðorð system, and see how far it answers to the old Norse

The Goði or Priest.

[n] Cf. Grágás § þingsk., cap. 58, 60, 61.

organisation. What, then, were the duties of the Goði, and what the nature and extent of his authority?

The duties of the Hofgoði were many and various. "His power and influence extended to every branch of what we should call the public service[o]." From the first they were of a twofold character; on the one hand religious, on the other secular or political, as is expressed in the following passage from the Landnámabók (iv. 7): "Then were persons chosen for their wisdom and uprightness, to tend the temple: they were to name judges at the þing and direct the course of justice (nefna dóma á þingum ok stýra sakferli); wherefore they were called goðar[p]." The religious duties of the Goði comprised care of the temple, and performance of sacrificial duties. He keeps the *stallahringr* or altar-ring, on which all oaths have to be sworn[q]. His it is *at helga þing*, to proclaim solemnly the sanctity

[o] Dasent, Burnt. Nj. 1, xlix.

[p] This passage refers to a later date, viz. Thord Gellir's Reforms; but it expresses fairly the duties of the Goðar.

[q] This ring answered to the Gospel book, which with us is kissed on taking an oath. According to Landnám, 4, 7, it is to be "of two ounces weight or more." In Viga Glum S. c. 25, "it must weigh not less than three ounces," and appears to have been of silver. It was the duty of the Goði to carry it with him to every meeting (til lögþinga allra).—Cf. Maur. Beitr., p. 86. One of the earliest references to the ring-oath is in the Edda, Hávamál, 110. "Baugeið Óðin hygg ek at unnit hafi, hvat skal hanns trygðum trúa?"—Glum's oath, which, however, was an exceptional case, is interesting in more ways than one, "vark at pár, ok vák ek þar ok raudkat þar odd ok egg." (cf. Head's Translation, p. 102, and Vigf. Dict. s. v. at.)

of a public meeting, and fix the þinghelgi or consecrated precincts. In his double capacity of "minister and magistrate," he presides over the assembly, which, it is to be remembered, met for many other purposes besides the transaction of formal business. He names the judges in law-suits, except so far as the litigant parties have to do so; and otherwise "steers" (styra) the course of justice. Further, as magistrate, he is supreme in his own district, and in this capacity he purges the land of all crime (*at hreinsa heraðʼ,*) and performs various duties pertaining now-a-days to coastguardsmen and custom officers. For example, he first goes on board strange ships which have put in, when he has the choice of any wares they may bring, and the privilege of fixing the price at which they are to be offered for sale. He has the power of forbidding the strangers intercourse with his Thingmen, and even of preventing them from landing at all: on the other hand, it falls to him to make arrangements for their proper accommodation and entertainment, the cost of which he also regulates. Thus, when Thangbrand arrived in the Berufjorð, the two brothers Thorleif and Kettle, dwelling at Berunes, "held a meeting and forbade men to have any dealings with him;" which when Hall of the Side heard, he rode to the ship with twenty-nine men, and invited the new-comer and all his men to his house, "running the risk of being able to get rid of all their wares for them." As a sort of consul, he affords strangers protection, at the same time looking to the interests of his countrymen in their international dealings. In the event of a foreigner's death by violence, his duty requires him to pursue the murderer; and in any case, he has the disposal of his inheritance. In hard times he looks after the poor, answering in this capacity to the "guardian" of modern times. To the duties of "Inland Revenue officer" he adds the cares of a "Minister of Agriculture," and like the "Prætor" in ancient Rome conducts the manumission of slaves.

But if his duties as a local magistrate and State minister were thus numerous and burdensome, his relations with his þingmenn (i.e. members of the þing community of which he is head) were such as to remind one of the paternalism of a feudal lord. He owes to them *traust*[r], i.e. protection and support; and they in turn are bound to give him lið, or service. The Goði represents the interests of all his Thingmen, who look up to him for protection and support in law-suits, &c.; and on the other hand, he can summon them to accompany him on many expeditions, and can always require a ninth part of them to attend him at the Althing. Such an extensive sphere of activity would naturally require much moving about from place to place,

[r] This word Dr. Maurer likens to the Frankish *trustis*. Cp. Hrafnkels, Saga, p. 24. "No one could remain at peace in the country, unless he asked Hrafnkels' permission. So they all agreed to give him their *liðsinni* (=lið), and he promised in return his *traust*. Then he subdued all the country east of Lagarfljót, and soon this þinghá (i.e. district) became much wider and more populated than before."

and we find in fact that he was to make progresses through his district, on which occasions his Thing-men have to attend him, if necessary, and entertain him on his journey[a]. So far from being a lucrative post, his many and various duties entailed, as might be expected, very considerable expenses; in reality, the office of Goði conferred *velldi enn eigi fé*, power not revenue. Hence the question as to whether any provision was made towards defraying his expenses. The chief source of his income was no doubt the *hoftollr*, or temple-dues, payable by each Thingman; besides which fees and fines of various kinds, life-money, legacy duties, and so forth, added a certain proportion; but all this together can hardly have been sufficient to defray the necessary expenses of his post. Hence, perhaps, the abuse of the practice of *arfsal*, a species of *clientela*, which will demand our notice in another connexion.

§ 16. The above examination brings to light the vast extent of the authority which the Goði in early times possessed; it was in fact "the sole existing authority," and when to this it is added that this ill-defined and all-embracing authority was unfettered by any geographical limitation, it may well excite surprise that no grave disorders arose from its abuse. Yet it is in this very fact that it was a *personal* and not a *territorial* relation that the remedy *Nature of his office and authority. Extent of his Jurisdiction.*

---

[a] In this, as in other respects (e.g. his claim on property for which no rightful heir is forthcoming), the comparison with the king of former days is obvious. After the fall of the Republic, these progresses were made by the royal lögmenn or syslumenn.

lay. The Thingmen of a Goði were not necessarily the inhabitants of his immediate neighbourhood, though no doubt this was, as a rule, the case. Any man might join or leave any Goðorð at will, (as reciprocally, a Goði might refuse admittance to his Goðorð, or turn a man out of it); and this liberty, though in all probability of little avail where a strong Goði was opposed to the secession of his Thingmen, yet acted as a check against the tendency to tyranny. On the other hand, a clever and popular Goði might secure Thingmen in every part of the island, it being the practice, after the establishment of a regular government, for the Thingmen, once a year at a public meeting to declare to what Goðorð they would belong [t].

The Lögmaðr.

§ 17. Alongside of the Goði there existed, from the earliest times, another officer [u], the *lögmaðr*, who

---

[t] This adherence to a Goði was called þingfesti, cf. Grágás þingskap, c. 58, &c. Schlegel, i. 158 sqq. See App. B.

[u] Mr. Dasent (Burnt. Nj., p. clxx., note), observes, that "the only point which Maurer seems not to have proved, is the existence of the lögmaðr as a regular official in each priesthood, and bearing in some respects a co-ordinate authority with the priests themselves." In the only two passages, he adds, on which the existence of such an official rests, it seems doubtful whether the term does not mean simply a skilled lawyer, like Njal or Mord. In the text, Maurer's conclusion from his Beiträge (p. 142; cp. p. 181, n. 6,) is given. In his most recent work, however, (Island., p. 211), he seems to have changed his first view, and writes, "Lögmaðr hiess hier (i.e. in' Icel.) nur der Rechtskundige als solcher, ohne irgendwelcher Beziehung auf irgend ein Amt." The same conclusion is supported by Mr. Vigfússon. The text has not been altered, because, though not a public officer, the lögmaðr (as in the case of Njal, who was not a Goði) exercised so important an influence, that a separate notice seemed desirable.

must not be overlooked, though the scantiness of our authorities leaves us in much doubt as to the exact position he held before the formation of the Commonwealth. His office was, as in Sweden (where he was elected by the people), and in Norway (where he was the king's nominee), to declare the law to the people, and give legal decisions on any point that was brought before him. Thus, as at first the laws were unwritten, the importance attaching to his office was very considerable. But whether in Iceland each Goðorð had its own lögmaðr, or whether the extent of his jurisdiction, in each case, corresponded with his personal influence and reputation, it is difficult to say. However this may be, two officers bearing this title, and acting as the king's representatives, superseded the lögsögumaðr (or President of the Republic) after the union with Norway, when they were said to *hafa bók*, hold the book or code.

§ 18. The close similarity between the primitive organisation of Iceland, as drawn out above, and the old organisation belonging to Norway, confirms the conclusion previously suggested, that the settlers reproduced, so far as circumstances would allow, the institutions of their old home. In either case there is a system of small independent lordships, whose rulers are at once priest and warrior, "minister and magistrate;" wielding an extensive authority over all departments of life, civil and religious. In either case, the connexion between the lay and the religious sides of the national life

Comparison of Iceland with Norway.

is clearly marked, and the hoftollr, or temple dues, which formed the revenues of the Icelandic temple, answered to the nefgildi or poll-tax, levied for the same purpose on the heraðs or fylkis of Norway.

But while in their social life and political institutions the Icelanders and Norwegians had so much in common, there were yet certain important differences, arising out of the different conditions which the new country imposed on the settlers. The territorial divisions of Norway were too intimately connected with its history and political organisation, to be transferred to a country where no state as yet existed, and whose whole history lay in the future. The straggling and haphazard manner in which the land was taken possession of, prevented any organised division into distinct geographical districts. It was not until much later that the organisation into Quarters and Things took place. Hence the graduated system of fylki and herað, which existed in Norway, found no place in Iceland; and whereas the authority of the Norse chieftains was confined within distinct geographical bounds, in Iceland on the other hand, it was, as we have seen, entirely personal, shifting and undefined. Again, the patriarchal manner in which the Goðorð system grew up, was the cause of its being regarded rather as *personal* property, which could be disposed of as any other such property would be; whereas in Norway the office of ruler was more like *real* property, which could descend only by inheritance, or be transferred by public election. Lastly, while in Norway the lay element predominates in the titles of the various classes of rulers, konungr, hersir, fylkir, &c.; in Iceland the religious title hofgoði is universal, and lasts long after the functions which it originally implied were abolished. As a further consequence, the same terms are used indiscriminately to designate the thing-community and the priest's jurisdiction; the hofgoði presides over his goðorð, or þingmannasveit or þinghá, the members of which are his þingmenn. So in the early Anglo-Saxon polity of England, the parish and tun-scipe were identical, the former being nothing more than the latter in its ecclesiastical aspect; for "just as the kingdom and shire were the natural sphere of the bishop, so was the township of the single priest; and the parish was but the township or cluster of townships to which that priest ministered[x]."

§ 19. Such, then, was the earliest condition of Iceland after the settlement. Form of government there was none. In the words of Mr. Dasent, "A number of little kingdoms had been formed all round the coast of Iceland, ruled by the priests, who at stated times convened their adherents and retainers to meetings, for the settlement of matters which concerned any or all of them. These were called things, mót-þings, or meetings. Each was independent of the other, and quarrels between the members of two separate Things could only be settled, as the quarrels of nations are settled, by treaty

Ulfljót establishes the Althing.

[x] Stubbs, C. H., i. 237.

or war." Such quarrels must have been very frequent, and constant collisions must have resulted in a state of incessant warfare. But such a condition of affairs could not last long; and so we find that in 927—930, some sixty years after the first settlers had arrived, one, Ulfljót by name, stood forth as lawgiver to the whole island, and drew up a constitution on the lines of the Gulathing laws. As to the circumstances which immediately led to this step nothing is told us. It would seem as if all the chiefs had come together, and acted collectively in the matter; and it would be interesting to know what were the circumstances under which they thus combined; but no clue remains, and conjecture is idle. One thing, however, is clear, that the chiefs must have been driven in sheer self-defence, by the anarchy which, there can be little doubt, reigned throughout the island, to concert measures for mutual protection.

Unhappily the larger work of Ari hinn Froði is lost, and our only authority (his epitome, the Islendingabók), is not very explicit on this subject. What it records, however, is worth reproducing. "Now when Iceland was fully colonised, an Easterling, Ulfljót by name, was the first to bring hither laws from Norway, and they were called Ulfljót's Code . . . They were for the most part arranged after the manner of the Gulaþing Code[y]: though

---

[y] "En þau vóro flest sett at því sem þá vóro Golaþingslög." The importance of the words "sem þá vóro" (as they then were), is pointed out by Schlegel, Grág. i. xviii., who shews that, in con-

Thorleif the wise was consulted as to what should be added, or taken away, or otherwise changed ᶻ." Then it goes on to relate how Grim, Ulfljót's foster-brother, travelled through the whole of Iceland on foot, in search of a proper site for the Althing ᵃ. The site at last chosen was a spot called Kol's grave, which, owing to a murder there committed, had been confiscated to the public use; "wherefore it was devoted to the Althing, and hence every one has now the right to fetch fuel from the woods, and pasture his horses in the meadows, during the parliament."

The Ulfljót Constitution marks an epoch in the history of Iceland, and forms as important a step in the progress of that country, as in Norway the establishment of monarchy had been. Hitherto

---

sequence of neglecting them, this passage has been taken to refer to the code of Hakon, foster-son of Athelstan, who, however, did not begin to reign till 934, or six years after the promulgation of Ulfljót's Constitution; cf. the Chronological Table.

ᶻ These words shew that a complete comparison of Icelandic with Norse law would be impossible; for next to nothing is told us of Ulfljót's legislation, and it is clear that he did not slavishly copy the Gulaþing Code.

ᵃ The Thingvalla, or site of the Althing, has been so accurately and minutely described by Mr. Dasent (B. Njal., cxxiii. sqq.), that any attempt at delineation of the spot, by one who has never visited it, would necessarily be mere repetition. A special interest, however, attaches to the *Lögberg*, or Hill of Laws at the Althing, and the þingbrekka or Parliament brink of other Things, where the law was read, speeches made, proclamations issued, &c., on account of the still-existing usage at the Tynwald, in the Isle of Man (cf. Vigf. s. v. *lögsaga*), which may be traced to the occupation of that island by the Northmen.

there had been no settled form of government; the country had been split up into so many entirely independent states. This deficiency was now remedied by the establishment of a national assembly —allsherjar, or al-thing—for the transaction of the judicial and legislative business of the whole island, which was to meet every summer for a brief session of fourteen days[b]. It is matter for regret that so little has come down to us as to the exact composition of the executive, as it originally existed in Ulfljót's constitution. The absence of any details renders it necessary to reason back from a somewhat later state of things to what probably existed in his time[c]. It is in the first place certain, that the same body exercised at once the judicial and legislative powers of the State. But in the absence of any authority, it is impossible to say whether these powers were assigned from the first to an executive committee—the Lögrétta—as was undoubtedly later the case; or whether, as in the Teutonic "Diets" of the Continent, the whole body of freemen were admitted to a share in the administration. The former is, at least, the more probable hypothesis; for the establishment in after times of

[b] According to Icelandic reckoning, when ten full weeks of the summer had passed; so that, says Mr. Dasent, the first day of the Althing would be somewhere about the 18th to the 24th of June. Cf. Islend., c. 7; Maurer, Isl., pp. 160, 162.

[c] Ulfljót was already sixty years old when he went to Norway for three years, to study the best form of government to be introduced into Iceland; and the date of the next reform is thirty years later. Cf. Maur. Beitr., p. 165.

a separate executive committee, would have involved a measure of disfranchisement hardly compatible with the principles of a free state. Whether the sole administration was in the hands of the Goðar or not, it is at least certain that they played the principal part in the Althing; and it is most probable that the appointment by them of judges (they themselves having no seat in the courts of justice) was a later reform, cotemporary with the separation of the judicial duties from the executive.

§ 20. The President of the Assembly thus constituted was the Lögsögumaðr [d]. He is to be elected at the Althing on a fixed day, before the declaration of the suits. If all men agree upon one man (so the law quaintly runs [e]), it is well. If not, it shall be decided by lot from which quarter the Lögsögumaðr shall be elected, and the inhabitants of that quarter shall then elect whom they will [f]. Special provision is made for his support. Every summer he is to receive 200 ells of vaðmal [g] out of the State

Of the Lögsögumaðr, or Speaker.

---

[d] The Allsherjargoði, or high-priest, (i.e. the Goði in whose Goðorð the Thingvalla lay,) was probably not made president, on account of the political objections to which such a selection would have been open.   [e] Grágás, i. 1.

[f] Ib. This law is clearly much later than Ulfjót's Constitution. For the division of the island into fjorðungar did not take place till 965. Apparently, before this date, no regulations were found requisite for the election of president. For hitherto it may be supposed that the election had been unanimous, as would be natural in a young society, where, perhaps, there was only one man distinctly qualified for the post. Besides, there had been only two elections. Cp. Chronological Table.

[g] i.e. woollen cloth of standard quality; our "wadmal."

revenues, and half the fines imposed by the Courts. After holding office for three summers, he shall in the fourth read out the þingsköp (rules of the parliament), and then, if he will, he may be released from his duties. If he prefers to be re-elected for a further term of office, he shall be elected by a majority of the lögrétta.

His duties, like those of the Norse lögmenn (of whom he was apparently a copy), were to proclaim the law (seggja upp lög), to the assembled Thing at stated intervals, viz. partly every year, partly every third year; to decide knotty points of the law referred to him for judgment[h], and generally to act as "Speaker" of the Parliament. "Speaker," indeed, is his most appropriate title; for in the modern Speaker of the House of Commons, we see the analogue of the Icelandic Lögsögumaðr; and hence it becomes all the more interesting to trace the functions which originally gave to the former his distinctive title, a title which, without the aid of Icelandic history, it would have been difficult to explain, or, in his present altered circumstances, to justify.

The care with which his power was hedged around, to check it from becoming too excessive, is noticeable. His term of office is limited to three years, though at the end of that period he may be re-elected; his post, though one of great honour, is strictly honorary,

[h] Skapti, Lögsögumaðr at the time of the great trial of the Burners, was frequently consulted during the trial by the two parties.

in the sense of conferring little influence beyond the limits of the Althing. In spite of this, however, a vigorous and influential Lögsögumaðr might wield a very real power, as is seen in the case of Skapti Thorodsson, " in whose days," says the author of the Islendingabók, (cap. 8), " many chiefs and nobles were condemned or banished for murder or bloodshed, by reason of his power and government[i]." During his three years of office, he was able, like the Roman prætors, to promulgate special edicts, which, however, were binding only during his term of office[k]. But it is clear that, when a popular Lögsögumaðr was often re-elected, and so held office for a continuous period of twenty years, (as did the second and third presidents,) his edicts would by custom become as binding as actual laws, and hence came to be written down along with the *statutes* in the Grágás. This explains the frequency with which the phrase *sem nu hefi ek tint*, " as I have now said," recurs in the code.

§ 21. The only alteration in the existing local administration that seems to have been effected, was the provision that cases of murder should in the first instance be brought before that court which

Political effects of Ulfljót's Reform, with reference to

---

[i] Islend., c. 8.
[k] An ecclesiastical law quoted by Schlegel (Grágás, xlii.), declares that "all laws shall be recited every three summers, at the end of which the Lögsögumaðr shall lay down his office. A new law shall not remain in force longer than three summers; and shall be recited the first summer from the Lögberg, at the Varthing lawfully constituted, or the Leið. All new laws shall be abrogated, if they are not recited every third summer."

the authority of the Goðar.

lay nearest to the spot, and that if the local authority should prove incompetent to decide the case, that it should then be brought before the Althing[1]. The consequences of this enactment will appear later. As a general result, it may be said that with the establishment of a Commonwealth, justice was, in theory at least, secured to all litigants, whether fellow-members of the same Goðorð, or Thingmen belonging to rival Goðar. It is unlikely that the individual Goðar were deprived of their local authority; but there can be no doubt that their former sovereign power was very much curtailed by the new order of things, though their loss in this respect must have been amply compensated by the fact that, in their collective capacity, they themselves formed the power that limited their individual action. It may not be unfair to compare them to Members of Parliament of the present day, who, in the House of Commons exercise their "Landsstjorn," and on the bench at Quarter Sessions perform the duties of the "Heráðsstjorn."

The Reforms of Thord Gellir.

§ 22. For a generation the new Constitution worked apparently without interruption, but at the end of that period, an event took place which revealed the weak point in its working, and was the immediate cause of the second great measure of reform in the history of Iceland, viz. the provincial organisation, which divided the land into Quarters and Things. In the year 964, a great suit arose between Thord Gelli and Tungu-Odd, in con-

---

[1] Cf. Islendingabók, c. 5.

sequence of the Blundketilsbrenna, or burning of Blundketill. Thord was chief prosecutor, and the case was brought before the local court of þingnes which was the nearest to the scene. But here the evil appeared, of having a case of this kind placed in the hands, as it were, of the guilty one, by bringing it before a tribunal where he in all probability reigned supreme [m]. The hostile parties came to blows, and blood was spilt, so that the court could not lawfully sit. At the Althing justice miscarried equally in the presence of the contending factions. Then Thord stood forth on the Hill of Laws, and referring to wrongs of his own which he had suffered, proposed his "Reform Bill," by which the land was to be divided into Quarters, "so that each Quarter should contain three Things, and the members of each Thing should settle all their affairs together; only in the Northern Quarter there were to be four Things, because they could not otherwise come to an agreement, ... though, in the nomination of Judges and constitution of the Lögrétta, the number was to be same as in the other Quarters [n]." Each Thing was to have its Varþing, or Spring-meeting, each Quarter its Quarter-meeting, while in the autumn, fourteen nights after the dissolution of the Althing, was held a Haustþing (Harvest-meeting), or Leið [o],—a "Court-leet," chiefly for the

[m] Even in later times, as appears from Laxdæla S. c. 82, it required no little courage, and was regarded as a great feat, to attempt to defend a suit in a strange court.

[n] Islendingabók, c. 5.

[o] From the Grágás, i. 122 (ed. Schl.), cap. 41, it appears that

purpose of informing the public of the new laws and licences of the recent Althing, to give out the calendar for the coming year, and so on. Further, each þingsökn, or County, was to comprise three þriðjungar, or "Ridings," being the three chief temples (höfuðhof) of the district, to be administered by goðar, priests, chosen for their personal character [p]. In the Althing itself, the legislature was separated from the High Court of Justice; and the latter was divided into four Quarter Courts (fjórðungsdómar), one for each of the new divisions or counties of the island. The judges of these courts were nominated by the Goðar, who themselves had no seats.

Such was the scope of Thord Gellir's Reform. Let us now consider, at somewhat greater length, the two divisions into which this great measure naturally divides itself.

<small>Division of Iceland into Quarters and Things.</small> (I.) The Division of Iceland into Quarters and Things limited the number of Goðorðs which had any influence on the government of the country

<small>the leið was held by the samþingis goðar at the same place as the varþing; but this was in the twelfth and thirteenth centuries. Mr. Vigfússon thinks that in the tenth century, "as may be inferred from the records of the Sagas, as also from local names indicating small county 'leets,' different from the samleið of Grágás," the leets were a kind of county assemblies. For derivation of the word, see App. C.

[p] So at least says the Landnáma, iv. 7. But the assertion can hardly be correct, for there are plenty of instances to shew, that in later times the Goðorðs remained as property in the hands of their former possessors; cp. Eyrb. Saga.</small>

to thirty-nine [q], though no doubt plenty of other Goðorðs existed, and new ones might always be founded. The relations of the Goði to his Thingmen were modified only so far as was necessitated by the union of three Goðar to form each þing: such unions being termed samþingi, and the three priests sharing this joint jurisdiction being called samþingis goðar. Hence, as the Goðorð remained a purely personal aggregation till the end of the Republic, the latter also, being merely combinations of individual Goðorðs, must have been equally personal, and not territorial divisions [r]. Such, however, was not the case with the fjorðungar or quarters, which from the first were distinct geographical counties; so that no one could be a Thingman to the Goði of one quarter, who himself resided in another quarter.

The evils complained of by Thord, and which the Blundketilsbrenna had brought into such prominence, were remedied by the substitution of the samþingi, or joint jurisdiction of three Goðar for the private court, formerly presided over by one Goði only. In this local court, which formed a sort of "court of first instance" for the district, twelve judges were appointed by each of the three presiding Goðar. Hence "the plaintiff or defendant

[q] Viz. 4 Quarters = 12 Things = 36 Goðorðs + 3 additional ones for the north quarter.

[r] Cf. Maur. Isl., p. 157. "Die rein persönliche natur des Goðorðs und damit auch der þingsökn, welche ja nur einen Complex mehrerer Goðorðe bildet, geradezu durch dessen geschichtliche Entwickelung bedingt ist."

might hope for a better chance of justice from an assembly presided over by several chiefs, than if he had to sue for it at the hands of one priest and his dependants, whom the very fact that gave rise to his suit had made his enemy [s]."

The new system of "County Courts" was so arranged as at once to expedite public business, and to afford as much chance as possible of an even administration of justice. Thus the institution of the Várthings, into which disputes between members of the same Thing should be brought, and of Quarter-things, in which suits between members of the same Quarter, but of different Things, should be tried, promoted a systematic distribution of judicial business, which prevented any wholesale accumulation of petty business in the higher courts, such as disfigures and impedes the administration of English Courts of Equity. The four Quarter Courts at the Althing, the highest courts in the country, dealt with disputes between litigant members of the different quarters, and at the same time constituted (until the erection of the Fifth Court) the High Court of Appeal. Into this court suits were brought, which had failed of decision in the lower provincial courts. It appears that it soon became the practice to appeal at once from the Várthing to the Althing; for our authorities shew that the Quarter-things presently fell into disuse [t], probably because it was

[s] Das. B. N., lxv.
[t] Very little indeed is known about the Quarter-things. Our authorities, almost unanimously, are silent with respect to them,

found that justice could more easily be obtained by an immediate appeal to the highest court.

(II.) A somewhat fuller discussion of the new Constitution of the Althing is needful, for upon a knowledge of its details is based a right understanding of the course of justice in Icelandic lawcourts, and of the further measure of reform which instituted the Fifth Court. As the basis of the Reform was the separation of the judicial from the legislative functions of the Althing, the constitution of the Lögrétta and of the Quarter Courts may most conveniently be considered separately. The section of the Grágás relating to the Althing provides as follows: "Three sets of benches shall be set round the Lögrétta, so that on each forty-eight men can conveniently be seated. Twelve men out of each quarter are to have seats in the Lögrétta, and, in addition to them, the Lögsögumaðr. They shall control all laws and licences. They are all to sit on the middle bench, where our Bishops also shall sit. From the north quarter, those twelve men shall sit in the Lögrétta who hold those twelve Goðorðs, which used to be held at the time when they had four Things, and three goðar in each Thing. But from all the other quarters nine men have seats, who hold the full, old (full ok forn) Goðorðs, three of which there used to be in each Várþing, when there were three Things in each

<small>Reform of the Althing.</small>

---

which shews how little they were used, or how soon they became disused. And the only reference to them in the Grágás seems to be under the section Vígsloði, c. 58, Schleg. i. xcii.

E

quarter. Now all these shall have one man beside them out of every ancient Thing, so that twelve men from every quarter shall have seats in the legislative assembly. Thus the ancient Goðorðs of the Northlanders are all curtailed in the arrangement of the Althing by one quarter in comparison with all other full Goðorðs throughout the land. Further, each of the men who, in this way, have seats in the Lögrétta, shall choose from among his Thingmen two men to sit beside him in the Lögrétta, and advise him, the one sitting in front, the other behind. And so shall all the benches be filled, and forty-eight men shall sit on each." Thus the whole Assembly would consist of 144 persons, exercising each an equal right of voting, forming with the Speaker of the Laws, who acted as President, a total of 145. To these in later times were added the two Bishops. The description extracted above from the Grágás applies, of course, to a much later date than the time of Thord Gellir now under consideration. But with the exception of the distinction between the "full ok forn" Goðorðs, and the more recently-erected ones, which distinction Thord Gellir's reform first introduced, there is nothing in the law, as above quoted, at variance with the state of things in his day.

Turning now to the constitution of the Quarter Courts, we find the following provision in the Icelandic Law : "Every Goði who has an old and full Goðorð shall name one man out of his Thingmen for the court." Thus each priest named from among his dependants four judges, one for each of the four courts. But from the northern quarter, which was not to have any privileges, three judges only were to be appointed by each Goði. This is not indeed stated by the law above quoted, but appears from other sources. If the number of judges appointed by the northern quarter was equal to those appointed by each of the other quarters, there would be an aggregate of 144, the same number as the members of the Lögrétta. Each court, too, would consist of the time-honoured "three twelves," about which in judicial matters there was a kind of special sanctity, such that when the Fifth Court was constituted so as to contain forty-eight judges, no decision was legal, if pronounced by more than thirty-six. Again, Skapti, whom Njál is consulting as to the Fifth Court, asks, "How wilt thou name a Fifth Court, when the Quarter Court is named for the old priesthoods, *three twelves in each quarter*[u]?" Lastly, the Islendingabók (c. 5) distinctly states that there should be no difference between the northern and the other quarters in this respect.

§ 23. The legislative and judicial administration formed only a portion of the business transacted at the Althing; the fourteen days during which it lasted were regarded as a general holiday; and men rode to Thingvalla, like Gunnar of Lithend, "to meet good and worthy men." All Franklins might go if they chose; while those were bound to appear, either in person or by proxy,

Meeting of the Althing.

[u] Njála, cap. 102, 143.

who had any public duties to perform, whether as Members of Parliament, neighbours, judges, or witnesses. Each person thus present in a public capacity (þingheyjandi, or þing-performer) received for his attendance a fee (þingfararkaup = fee for travelling to the parliament), which was defrayed by the Franklins who stayed at home. So the chiefs rode thither from all parts of the country with their households, attended by an armed retinue, a practice which, not unfrequently, led to severe fights on the way. Arrived at Thingvalla, each company arranged their booths, and along with the more serious business, all sorts of festivities and merry-making took place. While the elders talked over their business-matters, the state of trade, or the prospects of the coming harvest, the bachelor portion of the community would seize the opportunity of looking out for a wife, or indulge in the less hazardous pastimes of horse-fighting and other sports. Here, too, as at the great Olympic festivals of old, authors recited their new works to throngs of Hellenic listeners; so the Icelandic Scald would fix the attention of an excited audience, and call forth bursts of enthusiastic applause, by singing in animated strains the mighty feats of national heroes.

On the first evening, the Allsherjargoði, or high-priest, with solemn ceremonies hallows the assembly, and proclaims the consecrated precincts, within which even the outlaw was secure. Then every man must lay aside his arms, nor resume them until the last day of the meeting, when the Althing was dissolved (þinglausnir). After that, all took up at once their arms, and rode away to their homes. Hence the dissolution of the Parliament came to be called Vápnatak, a word whose significations are so diverse as to deserve a brief notice. In its earliest use, it signified the consent expressed by the armed freemen in the old Teutonic assemblies, by brandishing and clashing their weapons, a practice thus described by Tacitus[x]: "Si placuit sententia frameas concutiunt; honoratissimum assensûs genus est armis laudare." Hence it came to mean the decree thus ratified. The word passed, by what transition is not recorded, to the peculiar Icelandic use above noticed; and when next met with, it appears in a slightly different form (wæpentak) in our own land, where in the wholly new sense of a territorial subdivision answering to the Saxon *hundred*, it still remains a living witness of the Danish occupation.

§ 24. Before passing on to the next great measure of Reform, the erection of the Fifth Court, of which Njál was the author, and which formed the coping-stone of the Constitution, it is worth noticing, that the political effect of the present measure had a directly aristocratic tendency; and in this respect deserves comparison with that of Njál, which was intended as a check against the oligarchical party, and as a step in the direction of democratic reform. The influence of the Goðar with their

Thord Gellir's Reforms considered, with reference to their political results.

[x] Germ. 11.

Thingmen, and the numerous powers which they enjoyed, were little interfered with by the changes which had taken place. But, on the other hand, the immediate effect of the Thord Gellir "Reform Act," was to raise the ruling Goðar to a privileged position above their fellows, by limiting the numbers of those admitted to a share in the administration to thirty-nine. Nor does it appear that any compensation was afforded to the masses, over whom these ruling Goðar were thus exalted by popular election or otherwise. For the Goðar held their new position, as is expressly stated in the Grágás as cited above, from the fact of their having possession of Goðorðs at the time the reform was made. Any one henceforth, who wished to "stand for Parliament," must (as in the case of Hauskuld, the Priest of Whiteness), obtain one of the "old and full" priesthoods. "We say priesthoods," (to adopt Mr. Dasent's words), "because the office, by the subdivision of property, could now be held by several persons at once, though the state only recognised their acts as the acts of one. Again, though any one who had means and influence enough might still build a temple, and gather followers and Thingmen around him; *still his new temple would not be one of the recognised temples, and he would not be a priest in the sense required by the Constitution.*" Njál's reform, as will be seen later, necessitated the erection of new "parliamentary" Goðorðs; and it is, perhaps, not unfair to conjecture that his burning was not wholly unconnected with the antipathy which such an infringement of the rights of a non-privileged ruling-class must have excited against him [y]. It would, perhaps, be hardly correct, to assume that the formation of a privileged ruling oligarchy was aimed at by Thord Gellir. Rather, the opposition with which his scheme was met in the northern part of the island, through which four Things had to be established, instead of three,—"af því at þeir urðo eigi á annat sátter,"—and the compromise, for compromise it was, by which that obstacle was surmounted, indicate only too clearly the independence still possessed by the autonomous chiefs, and their dislike to any reform which should in any way threaten their power.

Other indications of the same feeling among the chiefs of the northern divisions of the island are found in later history. Thus Bishop Gizur devoted a fourth part of his bishopric to the erection of a second See, in obedience to the wishes of the Northerners, "svá sem Norðlendingar æstu hann til [z]." And again, when Queen Margaret of Norway attempted to levy taxes in Iceland, the following entry is found in the annals for the year 1393: "The 'Statholder' brought forward the Queen's de-

[y] Some countenance is lent to this hypothesis by the fact, that not long before the very stronghold of the power of the priests had been attacked by the introduction of Christianity, which Njál was one of the first to embrace; cp. Maurer, Isl., p. 66. "Für den alten Njál scheint die feindselige Haltung, welche er den alten Godenhaüsern gegenuber eingenommen halte, die Ursache seines Unterganges geworden sein."

[z] Islend., c. 10.

mand at the meeting, when all the chief men promised to give sixteen feet of *vaðmál*[a] for Vigfus' sake—he was very much beloved in Iceland; but on this condition, that it should not be called a tax, and should not be demanded again. *But the inhabitants of Eyafjorð refused to give anything.*"

Political crisis. Necessity for new reforms.

§ 25. Forty years after the passing of Thord Gellir's "Reform Bill," it had become only too apparent, that a new measure of reform was needed to save the country from anarchy and ruin. Imperfections in the Constitution were the cause of so grave a perversion of justice, that the people, despairing of obtaining verdicts in the Law Courts, had come to the conclusion that it was far simpler and easier to decide all cases off-hand by the sword. "We cannot get our suits settled," they cried, "at the Althing; why not seek our rights with point and edge[b]?" The Holmganga, or wager of battle fought on an islet or *holm*, had ever been recognised as a legitimate method of deciding disputes. Wherever a Thing was held, a place was set apart

---

[a] This was cloth used for barter, before coinage was introduced; cf. Robertson, p. 52. "In the opinion of the best authorities of the North, no coins were struck in Norway before the middle or close of the tenth century. Bullion must have passed before this time, and the earliest substitute for a coinage was *wadmal*;" on the several kinds of silver, cf. Grág. Vigsl., cap. cxiv., &c. The Northmen can hardly have introduced coinage into Ireland, as has been supposed; for says Mr. Robertson, p. 54,—"They were still in the age of bullion and wadmal, when they were ravaging the English and Irish coasts in the eighth and ninth centuries." On the other side cf. Worsaae.

[b] Cf. Njála, c. 102.

for such duelling, which was conducted according to fixed rites and rules^c, much in the same way as, in later times, the Norman wager of battel (which, no doubt, sprang from the holmgang) was regulated. In Iceland it was always open to a man to challenge his adversary to "trial by combat," instead of "trial by inquest," if he chose. So Gunnar of Lithend refused to plead, but chose rather to challenge Hrut, and so decide his suit. But at the time of which we are now speaking, owing to the necessity imposed upon the judges of returning an unanimous, or virtually unanimous verdict; and owing to the vast mass of legal technicalities, which had so overgrown the spirit of justice, that a single flaw even in the wording was enough to quash a pleading; owing, moreover, to the ever-contingent possibility of being defeated in a suit by chicanery, duplicity, and open violence, many important suits at the Althing were never decided at all; and thus the appeal to the sword was, as it were, forced upon the people by the law itself. Hence their determination to have done with law, and seek their rights rather "with point and edge." Thus a return to the anarchy and barbarism of a former age, before law and order had come into existence, was imminent.

In this grave crisis, Njál, the greatest of living lawyers in Iceland, came forward and counselled his countrymen. "It will never do," he said, "to

^c Quite an elaborate code of honour for duelling is to be found in Kormak's Saga, c. 10.

have no law in the land. Let us call together all the chiefs, and talk the matter over." Then Njál[d] laid before the Court of Laws the proposals by which he hoped to remedy the evils which threatened to overwhelm the country, and of which the people with justice complained. His principal proposal was the erection of a Fifth Court, or High Court of Appeal; but this was, in fact, only a portion of a much wider and more radical reform.

Njál proposes his Reform Bill.

§ 26. At the risk of proving tedious, we shall allow Njál to give his proposals in his own words, as rendered in Mr. Dasent's able translation. "Methinks," he says to the Council of Chiefs[e], "it were wiser if we had a Fifth Court, and there pleaded those suits which cannot be brought to an end in the Quarter Courts."—"How," said Skapti, "wilt thou name a Fifth Court, when the Quarter Court is named for the old priesthoods, three twelves in each quarter?"—"I can see help for that," says Njál, "by setting up new priesthoods, and filling them with the men who are best fitted in each

[d] In the Islendingabók, c. 8, we read, "Skapti hafðe lögsögo xxvii. sumor; hann sette fimtardóms lög.," i.e. Skapti held the office of Speaker twenty-seven summers. He passed the Fifth Court Law. This is not at variance with the Njála. The scheme was Njál's; but not being a Goði, he could, presumably, not "carry the bill through" himself. Skapti, as President, "brought the Fifth Court into the Law." Njál attended the sitting of the Lögrétta, probably, as Dr. Maurer remarks (Beitr., p. 181, n. 6), as the counsellor nominated by one of the Goðar; but not, following what has already (supr., § 17, n. u) been said, as Lögmaðr of his district, the alternative proposed by the same learned author.

[e] Das. Burnt, Nj. 2, 84. Sagan af Njál, cap. xcviii.

quarter, and then let those men who are willing to agree to it declare themselves ready to join the new priest's Thing."—" Well," says Skapti, " we will take this choice; but what weighty suits shall come before the court?"—" These matters shall come before it," says Njál; "all matters of contempt of the Thing, such as if men bear false witness, or utter a false finding; hither, too, shall come all those suits in which the judges are divided in opinion in the Quarter Courts. Then they shall be summoned to the Fifth Court: so, too, if men offer bribes, or take them, for their help in suits. In this court all the oaths shall be of the strongest kind, and two men shall follow every oath, who shall support, on their words of honour, what the others swear. So it shall be also if the pleadings on one side are right in form, and the other wrong, that the judgment shall be given for those that are right in form. Every suit in this court shall be pleaded as is now done in the Quarter Court; save and except that when four twelves are named in the Fifth Court, then the plaintiff shall name and set aside six men out of the court, and the defendant other six. But if he will not set them aside, then the plaintiff shall name them, and set them aside as he has done with his own six. But if the plaintiff does not set them aside, then the suit comes to nought; for three twelves shall utter judgment on all suits.

" We shall also have this arrangement in the Court of Laws, that those only shall have the right to make or change laws who sit on the middle bench, and to this bench those only shall be chosen who are wisest and best. There, too, shall the Fifth Court sit; but if those who sit in the Court of Laws are not agreed as to what they shall allow or bring in as law, then they shall clear the court for a division, and the majority shall bind the rest; but if any man who has a seat in the court be outside the Court of Laws, and cannot get inside it, or thinks himself overborne in the suit, then he shall forbid them by a protest, so that they can hear it in the court; and then he has made all their grants and all their decisions void and of none effect, and stopped them by his protest."

<small>Analysis of his Reforms. The Fimtardómr.</small> § 27. In the above account of Njál's reforms, as stated by himself, three distinct measures are proposed, each of which deserves separate consideration. First and foremost there is the Fimtardómr, established for the purpose of deciding all those cases which, for whatever reason, the lower courts have proved incompetent to deal with. Secondly, there is a proposed reform of the Lögrétta; and lastly, in view of the exigencies of the new Court of Appeal, the erection of a number of new Goðorðs is demanded.

The new Court of Appeal is to consist of forty-eight members; but as the time-honoured number of three twelves must give a verdict, the plaintiff or defendant, or both, must challenge and set aside six of the judges on each side; a provision which is also intended to secure greater impartiality. At the same time, the omission to thus set aside twelve of the judges constitutes a flaw in the proceedings, sufficient to quash the suit, as was the case in the trial of Flosi and the Burners. The increased sacredness and binding character of the oaths, and the necessity of having two Sannaðarmenn, or Soothmen, as also the decision by majority in the place of an unanimous verdict, all contributed to render the course of justice more certain, and to obviate the necessity of an appeal to arms; and such was the salutary effect of the new provisions, that, within a very few years of their becoming law, it was found possible formally to abolish the time-honoured Holmgang [f].

[f] For a description of the last duel, between Gunnlaug and Rafn, in 1006, cf. Gunnl. Saga, cap. xi. (ed. Hafn.), the notes to which discuss the date of the abolition. The friends of the combatants interposed, and, to Gunnlaug's indignation, pronounced the duel drawn, Gunnlaug having received a slight wound, and Rafn having shivered his blade. The next day, with general approval, duels were by law abolished. Sir E. Head (Viga Glum S., p. 120) thinks that Dr. Maurer has not established the causal connexion between the erection of the Fifth Court and the abolition of the Holmgang, and prefers to attribute it to the moral influence of Christianity. It is, no doubt, true, that the introduction of Christianity in A.D. 1000, as well as the Reform of 1004, may have contributed to the abolition of the Holmgang in 1006. But, on the one hand, the reform was avowedly made with a view to repressing the Holmgang; and on the other, it is incredible that the new religion (the negative character of which at that time is dwelt on by Dr. Maurer, Isl., 82—84) could have wrought such changes in so short a time. It may be added, that after the abolition of the Holmgang (as well as the heathen ordeal of creeping under a sod—*ganga undir jarðarmen*, which, however, was rather Norse than Icelandic), the Christians introduced the ordeal

Erection of new Goðorðs. Political consequences.

§ 28. But it seemed that the requisite number of judges to sit in this new court could not be supplied by the thirty-nine ancient Goðar. Hence the proposal to erect new Goðorðs, fraught with consequences of no little importance; such at least is the reason given in the Njála; and in this sense Mr. Dasent writes [g]: "As the number of witnesses, judges, and freemen, to serve on the inquest was already almost enough to exhaust the resources of the old priesthoods, it was resolved to erect new priesthoods, in order to find witnesses, judges, and inquests for the new court." But when the full importance of this radical change is apprehended, it becomes impossible to believe that it was necessitated merely by a want of judges, &c., who could, in all probability, have been nominated by the existing Goðar. What the real motives were which actuated Njál in making this proposal, it is difficult, in the absence of all certain information, to say. The gossiping charge made against him in the Njála (c. 98), of introducing a radical change into the Constitution, merely for the purpose of securing to his son-in-law a seat in the Althing, is, on the face of it, so improbable, and so inconsistent with the uprightness of the great jurist's character, that it is not worth considering. "There have been historians," it has been well said, "who could ingeniously explain great events by mean anecdotes

of bearing hot iron in the hand, *bera járn*, but it appears to have been very rarely used. (Cf. Vigf.)

[g] B. Nj., clix.

of personal interests; but it is more intelligible to ascribe great results to great thoughts." The change, it can hardly be doubted, had its origin in some deep political intention, suggested by the necessity of removing the crying abuses of which the people complained. Was this the idea of introducing a democratic element into the existing oligarchy; or was it, on the other hand, to strengthen and confirm the power of the ruling class? That the latter was, in fact, the ultimate result, will be shewn later on; but that the former was Njál's real intention, seems indicated by several considerations.

(I.) In the first place, it is hardly beyond conjecture, that the troubles arising from the failure of justice may have excited discontent against the ruling class, in whose hands lay the whole administration, and who would therefore be held responsible for all abuses thence arising; and that Njál may have offered himself as a sort of champion of this democratic element, to help the people to secure the reforms needed. That he did thus associate himself with the governed, and not with the governing class, is distinctly stated. "It will never do," he declared to the discontented masses, "to have no law in the land; *but yet ye have much to say on your side in this matter*, and it behoves us who know the law, and are bound to guide the law, to set men at one again, and restore peace." Njál, though the first jurist of his day, was *not* a Goði. Mr. Dasent adopts throughout the view that the measure was a popular reform, and thinks "that the priests who filled the Court of Laws, were terrified by popular clamour into yielding their assent so readily to Njál's scheme[h]." However this may be, it is clear from the story itself that discontent was rife amongst the people, and that Njál's Reform allayed that discontent.

(II.) Why, if no democratic reform was intended, should the almost unconstitutional plan of erecting new Goðorðs have been adopted, instead of the much more simple plan of entrusting the nomination of the new judges to the existing Goðar, which, it does not appear, would have been impossible? It was only some forty years since the Reform of Thord Gellir had fixed the number of Goðorðs, and based upon that number the organisation of the country. The erection of wholly new Goðorðs, possessing special powers, completely upset that organisation. It established a new class of rulers, equal in power to the old Goðar, so far as their heraðsstjorn was concerned, or rather, in that they were not like the samþingisgoðar, trammelled by any joint jurisdiction, superior to the latter, and thus possessing a position which would soon be coveted by numbers even of the established Priesthood.

(III.) The erection of these new Goðorðs might be calculated to break the overwhelming power of the oligarchy; for the increase in numbers would materially diminish their prestige, and break up that compact *solidarité*, on which an oligarchy chiefly relies for strength; and the example once set,

[h] B. Nj., clx.

the number of these new semi-privileged Goðar would go on steadily increasing. Further, the provision that the new Goðorðs should be formed by letting "those men who are willing to agree to it, declare themselves ready to join the new priest's Thing, was a terrible blow to the monopoly of authority enjoyed by the ruling families. The permission, always recognised by the law, for a Thingman to attach himself to whatever Goði he liked, had too probably been a mere theory, which could seldom have been put into practice." Now, however, the principle was re-asserted, and made a fact; and thus the heart of the power of the Goðar,—the exercise of their local authority,—was attacked.

§ 29. But the above view seems to receive additional confirmation from the reforms which Njál proceeded to apply to the legislative assembly. In the first place, all decisions were to be by the vote of the majority; next, the power of protest was given to a Goði, by which he could, if a case was being conducted unfairly, or if he was unjustly excluded from a division, quash the proceedings by uttering his veto. Lastly, the Goðar sitting on the middle bench, alone were to have the right of voting, the occupants of the other benches having only a "consultative" authority. But it was enacted (and this provision contains the gist of the whole matter), "to this middle bench those only shall be chosen, who are wisest and best." It is this last measure, the alteration of the voting-power in the Althing, which is the most important (the two first

Reform of the Lögrétta.

changes being merely technical), but at the same
time the most difficult to estimate; for nowhere are
we told by what kind of election "those who are
wisest and best" are to be chosen, whether by
popular electors, or only by a process of "coöpta-
tion," among the Goðar themselves. In the former
case, the political importance of the measure, as
a democratic reform giving a certain representa-
tion to the masses, cannot be exaggerated; in the
latter, it resolves itself into a *moderate extension of
the franchise* to a larger number of the Goðar[i].
Dr. Maurer, in his earlier work, inclines apparently
to the former view; he insists at any rate on the
fact of the reforms being directed against the
ruling aristocracy. But in his most recent work[j]
he concludes in favour of the latter view, on the
ground that it agrees, on the whole, better with the
story. Further than this, it is perhaps unsafe to
go, or to suppose that Njál would have ventured
upon so extreme a measure as the first supposition
would have involved. But it is open to question,
whether, in this case, the ruling families could, in
the face of the public discontent, have made that
determined resistance to the measure, which sealed
once for all the fate of all democratic tendencies,
riveted more firmly than ever the despotism of the

[i] This, it may be said, would have been the case, if the new
Goðar were permitted to vote. It is hardly probable that the
election would have been left entirely in the hands of the old-
established Goðar; for it is not easy to see how this would
have altered the *status quo*, as they would naturally have elected
themselves. [j] Island., pp. 207—210.

oligarchs, and eventually led to one of the principal causes of the downfall of the Republic.

§ 30. For Njál's reforms were not fully carried out, and precisely that portion of them was dropped which would have proved most salutary. The ruling Goðar gladly disfranchised the inner and outer benches from exercising the right of voting; nor did they resist the erection of new Goðorðs. But they stoutly refused to subject themselves, the occupants of the middle bench, to the hazard of an election, whether close or otherwise. And so, by a clever parry of the blow aimed at their authority, they succeeded in securing themselves against all further attack. The new Goðorð system was not, indeed, without fruit; for it tended gradually to the dissolution of the compact power of the oligarchy. The result, however, was not an extension of power on democratic principles, but an accumulation of Goðorðs in a few hands, and a consequent enhancement of the power of a few oligarchical families, which tended to the overthrow of the Republic, as the concluding part of this Essay will attempt to shew.

Njál's intentions frustrated.

PART II.

ICELANDIC LAW.

Importance of Icelandic law.

§ 31. THE gradual growth and development of the Icelandic Commonwealth has now been traced from its origin in the patriarchal sovereignty of the various chiefs who settled in the country, to its culmination in the reforms of the great lawyer Njál. Henceforth no further additions of any consequence were made to the edifice[a]. The building was complete, and, in the vigour of its youth, successfully resisted an attempt at annexation made by the King of Norway. But as years rolled on, the absence of that vitality and expansive growth which marks a free Republic, and the increasing limitation of power to a few ruling families, combined with the violent feuds between Church and State, which destroyed the stability and sapped the foundations of both, hastened the decay of freedom, and contributed to the ultimate submission of the island to the Crown of Norway in 1264.

Before proceeding to the consideration of the causes of this decline, an examination of the legal procedure of the Icelandic people seems desirable,

---

[a] For the writing down of the law in 1117, which met with the unanimous approval of the country (Islendingabók, c. 10), cf. App. A. Of the new codes introduced after the union with Norway, 1272—1281, it is unnecessary to speak here.

not only on the ground of its intrinsic interest, and the large place it occupied in their history; but even more, because the germs of legal, as of political institutions, being common to the several members of the Teutonic family, it is useful to trace and contrast the various development of those common germs, in obedience to the principles, and as influenced by the conditions, peculiar to each.

§ 32. What especially arrests the attention of the reader of the Sagas is, the vast number and variety of law-suits with which the old Icelanders occupied themselves, as well as their extreme reverence for legal forms and technicalities of procedure; which was such, that the slightest formal flaw was sufficient to quash the most important cases. This sentiment affects their whole literature, both prose and poetry, and is intimately connected with their every passion and feeling. The fact here noted appears the more strange, when it is remembered that the condition of the country was by no means one of peace and quietness. On the contrary, "Bloodshed and violence," as Sir E. Head remarks, "are common, and a man's consideration in the community depends mainly on his courage and wealth." The explanation of this apparent paradox—idolatry of the forms of legal procedure, accompanying a semi-barbarous condition of society—has been given by Sir H. Maine[b]. It is, he says, a natural phenomenon. An examination of the various an-

Idolatry for forms of legal procedure.

---

[b] In a lecture delivered in Oxford, Feb. 10, 1877.

cient codes of the Aryan race points to the conclusion, that in these early times the authority of the Law Courts exercised a sort of fascinating influence over men's minds, because they stand as the alternative to bloodshed and violence; and even in the earliest states of society, peace must prevail over war, else society itself would cease to exist. Hence, in the ancient codes of India and of Ireland, as well as in the Twelve Tables of Roman Law, we find the first and most prominent position accorded to the Courts of Justice [c]. Again, it has been noticed that, as soon as an ill-governed province in India comes under British rule, a vast influx of business into the Law Courts takes place, thus shewing the anxiety of the natives to settle their disputes by peaceable rather than by warlike means. On the other hand, as a nation advances in civilisation, its habits become more formed to law, and the reverence of an earlier age for legal forms decline. In the England of to-day, as in Athens of old, there

[c] Another point in connexion with Icelandic Criminal Justice is worth noticing, as affording additional confirmation of this community of ideas in the ancient codes. Sir H. Maine has pointed out, that, next to the forms of legal procedure, the most prominent position is assigned to *Theft*, as was natural under the then existing conditions of society. Iceland was no exception to this rule. The þjófr, or thief, was particularly detested, and no mercy was shewn to him, theft being punished by hanging; just as sheep stealing was a capital offence in England till half-a-century ago. A "thief's eyes" is synonymous with "an evil look;" as Hrut says of his little niece Hallgerda,—"But this I know not, whence Thiefs' eyes are come into our family." [Njála, c. 1. Cp. Vigf. Dict., s. v. þiófr.]

are seated in the national character habits of unquestioning observance of law, which cause an unconscious obedience to prevail.

Iceland, in the days of the Commonwealth, had not yet attained to this more advanced stage. But the personal participation by every freeman in the administration of justice, and the share which each enjoyed in the making and execution of the laws by which he was governed, had already done much to mature those principles of Constitutional freedom which few of the nations of Europe still possess; and, even at this early period, Iceland presented a favourable contrast to the feudal governments of a later age.

§ 33. The most characteristic feature of Icelandic legal procedure, the trial by búakvíðr, or inquest of neighbours, had its origin in the sense of freedom and personal independence, characteristic of the northern character, which taught them so early the art of self-government. If a man is killed, or in any way injured, no appeal, in the first instance at least, is required, to the supreme authorities of the state; no public prosecutor comes forward to claim justice on behalf of the crown, and to resent and punish the crime, as an injury against the head of the state. The cause of the injured man is taken up by himself or his nearest relatives, and either the matter is settled by the friendly arbitration of a third and independent party, or it is referred for decision to a private court of neighbours. Such a method of proceeding naturally belongs to the

[marginal notes: Principles on which Icelandic Law is based. Duty of revenge. Weregild. Holmganga.*]*

period when the evils of open violence were becoming fully recognised, and when, therefore, the desire for bloodthirsty revenge was less frequently yielded to. Revenge with the Northman was a duty[d]; but along with this sense of duty was the right of property, which, it was felt, all heads of families had in their kinsmen. Hence, if a man chose to forego his right of revenge, and refused to follow up the death of his kinsman by a blood feud, he would still deem it his duty to recover compensation for that loss of property which he had thereby sustained[e]. Hence arose, as Mr. Dasent points out[f], "those arbitrary tariffs for wounds or loss of life, which were gradually developed more or less completely in all the Teutonic and Scandinavian races, until every injury to life and limb had its proportionate price, according to the rank which the injured person bore in the social scale[g]." This private right of revenge, though it came to be

---

[d] Cf. Tac. Germ. 21. "Suscipere tam inimicitias seu patris seu propinqui quam amicitias necesse est; nec implacabiles durant. Luitur enim etiam homicidium certo armentorum ac pecorum numero," &c. The bonds of kinship and brotherhood, among the Scandinavians, were especially strong, each family forming *a kind of confederacy or fellowship, equally bound in rights and duties.* (Cp. Vigf. s. v. *frændi*.)

[e] This was the mannbætr or weregild; which is really the same as manngjöld (= bætr, Engl. *boot*), were being verr = man; cp. the law-phrase, *bata baugum* = pay weregild.

[f] B. Nj., xxxi.

[g] In illustration of the antiquity of the practice, Mr. Hallam (M. A., i. 207), aptly quotes the disputants represented on the shield of Achilles, wrangling before the judge, εἵνεκα ποινῆς ἀνδρὸς ἀποφθιμένου. (Il. Σ. 498).

superseded by suits at law for money compensation, was yet always recognised as underlying all forms of legal procedure, and in the form of Holmgang or Duel, might always be resorted to in cases where a party was displeased with the conduct of a suit. So Gunnar of Lithend, in the Njála, refused to proceed with a suit against Hrut, but adopted in preference the surer method of challenging the latter to single combat. At the same time, this trial by wager of battle was always regarded as in a manner contrary to law: it was contrasted with the procedure með lög; and as a rule, whenever possible, efforts were made to obviate it by arbitration and atonement. A good illustration of this fact is furnished by the scene in the Njála (cap. 56), where the same Gunnar, who is at law with Geir the Priest, forbids his adversary to proceed with his suit, and adds, "Besides, I will tell thee something else which I mean to do." "What," says Geir, "wilt thou challenge me to the island as thou art wont, and *not bear the law?*"—"Not that," answered Gunnar; "I shall summon thee at the hill of Laws, for that thou calledst those men on the Inquest, who had no right to deal with Audulf's slaying."

§ 34. But setting aside this more violent method of settling disputes, and confining our attention to the legal procedure, we see the principle above noticed of settling disputes, wherever possible, without appealing for aid to the state, realised in the private courts, which play so important a part

The Búakviðr or Inquest of Neighbours, based on the principle of self-government.

in the administration of justice; and to which, Dr. Maurer even says [h], the public courts were at first only subsidiary. This system was doubtless a development of the early patriarchal forms of administration, in which judicial as well as religious functions pertained to the priest. But the principle could not have been carried out except for the further feeling, that it was the duty of neighbours to afford one another all the support they could; and the Commonwealth, as the same author has remarked, "at first expected of its members a large display of 'self-government,' and imposed the duty of mutually lending extensive help, upon those who were neighbours together [i]." The reason for this apparently was, that whereas in Norway any man had the right of summoning a Thing if he wanted it, in Iceland, on the contrary, owing probably to the physical conditions of the country, where judicial Things met only at stated intervals, a man must summon his neighbours to act as a private court. Thus they were called together in numerous cases, and for all manner of purposes, where a man had any lýsing or declara-

[h] Island., p. 390. "Insoweit war dann die Stellung der Dinggerichte zu den Privatgerichten Zunächst eine *subsidiäre*," &c.

[i] Ib., p. 392. Quite in this spirit writes Prof. Stubbs, i. 608: "The institution of the jury was itself based on a representative idea; the jurors, to whatever fact, or in whatever capacity they swore, *declare the report of the community as to the fact in question.*" These words, though referring to the English jury system, are in perfect accord with Mr. Dasent's description of the Icelandic law-suit, as being "based on the evidence of the community, supported by oath." B. Nj., cxliii.

tion to make. But in such cases they played only the part of spectators or auditors; whereas in the cases which are about to come under our notice, where a man summons his neighbours to act as an Inquest for the purpose of proving any matter, their rôle is by no means a subordinate one.

The technical name for a Verdict or Inquest in Iceland was kvíðr[k]; and setting aside the fanga-kvíðr, or inquest taken at random, which scarcely ever occurs, two forms of inquest claim attention, viz., the búakvíðr or neighbour verdict, and the tólflarkvíðr or verdict of twelve. The latter consisted of a body of men, of whom eleven were to be summoned by the Goði of the district: and he, being the twelfth of the number, had to deliver the verdict. Hence it is also called Goðakvíðr, or priest-verdict. It was only appointed for certain cases defined by the law[l], and was probably not so popular as the búakvíðr, for from the Grágás it appears that the influence of the "foreman" Goði usually decided the vote, as was the case in the trial described in Viga Glum's Saga, ch. 18. The búakvíðr, as being closely akin to the English jury *de vicineto*, is the more important of the two, and intrinsically the most interesting. As the principle was to take a number of neighbours, either five or nine, residing in the immediate neighbourhood of the spot where the action took place, such inquests

[k] Kvíðr originally meant 'a saying,' 'saw,' hence 'verdict;' and is derived from kveða = to say, not from kvedja = to summon.
[l] e.g. Grágás, ii. 37; Vigsl., 22.

are differently designated as *reltvangsbúar*, or neighbours of the *locus actionis* (being the space within a bow-shot of the place all round), *engibúar*, or inquest to decide the possession of a meadow, sitting on the spot; *heimilisbúar*, or homestead neighbours, summoned from the same house, and so forth. They must be householders; in many cases only landed proprietors can serve, and very rarely *griðmenn*, or lodgers. In most cases they had to be summoned at home (kvedjabña heiman); but in certain exceptional cases, at the parliament (á þingi, þingkvöð), e.g., when one of the neighbours summoned had died, and it was necessary to supply his place, they must be summoned by the person who desires the inquest. They are strictly a means of proof for or against the accused; and are bound to do justice to both disputants, and decide on their own knowledge of facts, not on evidence adduced before them by other witnesses. They are, in fact, "jurors and witnesses in one." The necessity for taking the *nearest* neighbours to the spot (which was so imperative, that an inquest could be rejected if proved not to be so,) may be traced, with much probability, to the law, which defined a slaying as manslaughter and *not* murder, if notice thereof had immediately been given *at the next or at least at the third house*. In a sparsely inhabited country like Iceland, such a provision was doubtless necessary.

Private Courts of Justice. § 35. These neighbour inquests are in no wise to be confounded with the *sáttarmenn* or umpires, appointed to arbitrate a case. On the contrary, they form regular, though private courts, in contradistinction to the Thing, or public court; and as such the proceedings are conducted therein in precisely the same manner as in the public courts. Hence they are called *dómar;* and we read e.g. of *engidómr,* the same as engibúar, *afréttar dómr,* court for deciding causes relating to common pastures; *skuldadómr,* or court of payment for liquidation of debt on a person's death, and others of like kind. Contrary to the practice in the public courts, where, as has been shewn, the Goðar appoint regular judges, the contending parties themselves name the judges in these temporary or impromptu courts. They, too, fix the spot on which the court shall sit; there being in all this not the slightest state interference.

In case of *véfang,* (or, division of the court, when no decision was arrived at,) or, *Domsafglapan,* (contempt of court, disturbance of the proceedings by violence, brawling, crowding, &c.,) the case would be carried before one of the public courts, as also might be done from the first on the motion of the plaintiff. After the institution of the public courts, the criminal cases were probably, as a rule, carried at once before them, though the bulk of the civil process remained, no doubt, in the hands of these private courts. Their speedy decay is to be attributed, not to the immediate effect which the dwarfing influence of the new public courts might be supposed to have exercised over them, but rather to the dangers with which a powerful and arrogant adversary in a suit might at any time threaten the course of justice; dangers from which, indeed, even the higher courts were not free; but to which, in the absence of any public authority, the private courts must have been peculiarly liable.

Murder and manslaughter in Iceland.

§ 36. The present seems a fitting occasion for noticing the theory which prevailed in Iceland with respect to murder. The distinction which Icelandic Law drew between actual murder and manslaughter is not only eminently characteristic of the moral feeling of the race, but is besides interesting as a contrast to the principle on which a distinction is made in English law between those crimes. A man was guilty of murder (morð), if after killing a man he did not openly proclaim himself (lýsa vígi víglýsing) at the next, or at least, at the third house he passed, as the perpetrator of the deed [m]. It was also murder to slay a man at night (nátt-víg em mordvíg), or by any sort of treachery, or even if the víglýsing was stealthily performed; for "þat er morð ef maðr leynir eða hylr hræ ok gengr eigi í gegn," (i.e. if he hides or buries the corpse, or does not avow, lit. go to meet, the charge [n]). In all these cases the murderer was called morðvargr, and outside the pale of the Law. If, on the contrary, the slayer confessed what he had done, the act was only manslaughter (víg); and he was liable to a

---

[m] This provision is contained in the Gulaþing code. "The slayer shall not ride past any three houses, on the day he committed the deed, without avowing the deed, unless the kinsmen of the slain man, or enemies of the slayer live there, who would put his life in danger."   [n] Grág. Vigsloði, cap. xlix.

legal indictment; but the matter might be arranged by the prosecutors and relations of the deceased for payment of a certain weregild. The sagas are full of such slayings, which are indeed among the most usual occupations of the fiery Icelanders. Mr. Dasent adds that, "To kill a foe, and not bestow the rights of burial upon his body by throwing sand or gravel over him, was also looked on as murder [o]." If this be so, the community of ideas between the Icelander and the ancient Greeks and Romans is interesting, for exactly the same *sentiment*, of crime involved in the neglect to bury, is expressed in the lines of Horace :—

" Quanquam festinas (non est mora longa): licebit
  Injecto ter pulvere curras [p]."

This distinction is clearly based on that innate hatred of all dishonest, underhand and lying proceedings, in that love of open, straightforward dealing, which was the most marked characteristic of the Scandinavian race. "Even in killing a foe," as Mr. Dasent well expresses it, " there was an open, gentlemanlike way of doing it, to fail in which was shocking to the free and outspoken spirit of the age."

§ 37. The English criminal code, on the other hand, has for its basis the motives which impel a man to commit the crime. "Intention is in every case essential to crime [q]." If a man kills another

Comparison with English Criminal Law.

---

[o] B. Nj., xxxiii.   [p] Carm. i. 28.
[q] I. F. Stephen, "Criminal Law," p. 81. This is a quite modern

out of malice prepense, in a deliberate, cold-blooded manner, he is guilty of murder. But his crime is reckoned as manslaughter only, if it is proved in his favour that he was so influenced by other causes, (e.g. insanity, &c.,) as to be blind to the consequences of his conduct[r]. Hence a further difference between the criminal code of Iceland and that of England, viz. the simplicity of punishment in the former compared with the complexity of the latter. In Iceland, the question at issue in a trial for murder would have been, "Did the defendant or not slay this man, and having done so, did he or not avow the act, as the Law required?" a question which would easily be decided by the evidence of the búakviðr, who, being the nearest neighbours, must needs know. If he was convicted of murder, the sentence was clear, outlawry and banishment for a certain term of years. If convicted of manslaughter only, he was condemned to pay the necessary weregild, or, in default, to become an outlaw. Hence Icelandic law obviated the difficulties of apportioning the punishment to the degree of guilt, which the later system involves. The scale of punishments for greater or less offences in English law finds a par-

---

notion. In the heathen morals (and even in the Old Testament) *foolish* and *wicked* are kindred words, e.g. *glópr* = a fool; *glæpr* = an evil deed.

[r] "When one man kills another, the presumption is that he did so maliciously, and so committed murder. But this presumption may be rebutted by shewing that the act was done in self-defence, or under certain provocation, or by certain forms of negligence."—Ib., p. 83.

allel in the scale of the weregild for different classes of persons in the law of Iceland.

§ 38. It has been remarked that the Icelandic law did not aim at taking a man's life, and hence banishment was the most usual punishment for great crimes. But capital punishment was not therefore unknown or unpractised, at least, in the heathen age; for we find the executions of modern times represented by the *sacrifice* of criminals, as well as of slaves; a passage in the Biskups saga (i. 23,) mentions that "the heathen sacrifice all the worst men," a practice referred to seemingly in the following passage from Landnáma, 98 : "There stands Thorstein ..... near that judgment ring ('bar'), in which men shall sentence to death." . So, too, it would seem that thieves were hung. *[Capital Punishment in Iceland.]*

§ 39. But, whenever possible, friendly umpires (Görðarmenn) stepped in, and sought to bring about an atonement between the contending parties. Such courts of arbitration were very much used, even to settle matters of the highest importance, e.g. the introduction of Christianity, A.D. 1000, and, as Mr. Vigfússon has remarked, suited well the sagacious and law-abiding spirit of the people. Even the Sjálfdæmi, or self-doom (when one party gave it over to his adversary to give judgment himself), was a kind of arbitration. In modern Icelandic law, arbitration has become even a more essential mode of procedure than it was in former times; for, in all but criminal cases, the disputants have to appear before two or more forlíkunarmenn, or peace- *[Of Arbitration and Atonements.]*

G

makers, who are usually the clergyman and some of the chief men of the parish; nor may the case go before the courts, until such arbitration has been tried and failed. At first sight, this sensible system looks like a development of the ancient form; but Mr. Vigfússon thinks the practice was borrowed from Denmark. In this respect, Icelandic procedure offers one more point of comparison with the ancient Athenian law, where arbitration held a conspicuous place, as may be gathered from the following reference by Pollux (viii. 126), $\pi\acute{a}\lambda ai$ $o\dot{v}\delta\epsilon\mu\acute{\iota}a$ $\delta\acute{\iota}\kappa\eta$ $\pi\rho\grave{\iota}\nu$ $\dot{\epsilon}\pi\grave{\iota}$ $\delta\iota a\iota\tau\eta\tau\grave{a}s$ $\dot{\epsilon}\lambda\theta\epsilon\hat{\iota}\nu$ $\epsilon\dot{\iota}\sigma\acute{\eta}\gamma\epsilon\tau o$ (i.e. into the public courts).

When an atonement (grið or tryggð [s]) had thus been brought about by friendly intercession, the two parties were completely reconciled, and took oaths never to hurt each other more. In the formula of atonement, too, conditions were often imposed on the parties, e.g. exile for a term of years, or payment of fines. On the heads of those who, thus atoned, failed to comply with the conditions of the truce (griðniþingr), the heaviest curses were imprecated. They became utterly disgraced and accursed, and might be slain at any moment by their enemies. He is a truce-breaker (so runs one old *griðsmál* [t]) who breaks his atonement: let him be abhorred, and driven away of God and of all good men. In the

---

[s] Grið and tryggð are not, however, synonymous. The latter expresses a complete reconciliation; the former, a truce only for a definite period, which usually permitted the preliminaries of the tryggð to be arranged.   [t] Grág. 112.

Grágás, a number of griðsmál, or formulæ of atonement, are preserved, of which the following is selected as a fair specimen, embodying all the characteristics of the solemn ceremony, and suggesting an interesting comparison with some feudal practices of the middle ages:—

"Disputes arose between N. and M.: but they have now been settled and atoned for, and money paid; according as the meters meted it out, and the judges judged, the tellers told, the givers gave, the takers took, and carried off thence with them the full sum in lawful tender, which has been handed over to those who should take it. Ye shall be set at one and live friendly together, at meat and at drink, in the Althing and at meetings, at kirk prayers and in king's palace; and in whatever place else men meet together, there shall ye be so set at one, as if this quarrel had never come between you. Ye shall share knife and meat together, and all things besides, as friends and not as enemies. But if there shall be strife between you, then shall fines be paid, but blade shall not redden. But if one of you be so mad that he breaks the truce thus made, and slays after pledges have been given, he shall be an outlaw accursed and driven away, so far as men drive wolves furthest away. He shall be banished of gods and of all good Christian men, as far as Christian men seek churches, as heathen men sacrifice in temples; as mothers bring forth, son calls mother; flames blaze up, mankind kindle fire; earth is green, shield gleams, sun shines, and snow covers the ground; as far as Finn glides on snow-shoes, firs grow, and falcon flies the livelong summer day, borne up by a fair wind beneath both wings; wherever the heavens turn, the world is dwelt on, the wind blows, waters roll on to the sea, and karls grow corn. He shall flee from kirk and Christian men, God's house and mankind, from every home save hell. Now is the fine laid upon the book, which N. pays for himself and for his heirs, begotten and not begotten, born and unborn, named and unnamed; and M. on the other hand receives from N. pledges for ever and aye, which he shall keep, so long as world endureth, and men are living. Now shall they be set at one and at peace, wheresoever they may meet, by land or by water, on ship or on skate, on sea and on saddle, so that they share the pump-watch together, thwart or thole, knife or steak, as the case shall serve. Be ye set at one with one another, as father and son, or son with father. Join now your hands together, and be of one mind; as God and all the Saints witness, and all those men who have heard this peace-making."

The curious blending together of heathen and Christian ideas in the above, points at once to its origin and its antiquity. In the rude age of the early Icelanders, such solemn reconciliations must have exercised a very beneficial influence, by checking the savage blood-feuds, which otherwise would have been prolonged for generations, and which frequently only ended with extirpation from the island of all the kinsmen of one side or the other. To take a singe instance: in the Njála we have ample evidence of how one slaying leads on to another, until whole districts are animated with the same deadly feud, resulting in some dire catastrophe.

§ 40. Let us now look a little more closely into the conduct of a law-suit before one of the Quarter Courts. And for this purpose we may select the celebrated trial of "Mord v. Flosi," which forms the last act of the terrible tragedy, which has given the title of "The burning of Njál" to one of the most fascinating of the Icelandic Sagas. For though many other cases come before the reader of the *Njála*, this is the only one which is given in all its details, and which was conducted through all its stages at length, until the "Battle at the Althing" brought the legal proceedings to a bloody termination: the whole tendency of Icelandic legislation being, as Mr. Dasent says, "not to put forth the full force of the law, but rather to make matters up."

The Icelandic Law-suit. Preliminary proceedings.

An eminent lawyer, Mord, Valgard's son, has been retained to conduct the suit. For pleading before the Althing in those days required no less knowledge, skill, and ability than is required of a counsel in Westminster Hall to-day[u]. Besides

---

[u] Certainly less legal knowledge could not have been required in those days, when the Lögsögumaðr could use the following words:—"More men are great lawyers now than I thought: I must tell thee, then, that this is good law ... but still I thought that I alone would know this, now that Njál was dead, for he was the only man I ever knew who knew it." [Das., B. Nj., ii. 255.] And

(as will be noticed presently), the meaner portion of the community were glad to secure the protection of the great men, and put into their hands law-suits, which the latter, in their turn, were only too willing to conduct, on account of the popularity and prestige which accrued to them therefrom. He enters upon the first stage of the suit, by summoning nine "near neighbours to the spot" (*vetrangsbúas*), before whom he takes witness (*nefna vatti*) that the prosecutor has handed over to him this suit by law, "with all those proofs (sóknargögn) which have to follow the suit, to plead and to settle, and to enjoy all rights in it, as though I were the rightful next of kin." A second time he names his witnesses, to bear testimony that due notice is given of the cause of the suit, which must be described with all accuracy and in due order of details. In the Njál case, Mord gives notice of "an assault laid down by law (lögmætr frumhlaupi) against Flósi, Thord's son, for that he dealt Helgi, Njál's son, a brain or a body or a marrow wound, which proved a death wound. I give notice of this before five witnesses—and he named them all by name." Then witness is taken that this

---

considerably more nerve and presence of mind must have been required for addressing a vast assembly, which (as in the Athenian ἐκκλησία and δικαστήρια) greeted every point that was made with roars of applause or the reverse, than for addressing a British jury in a court, where every outburst of laughter or applause is rigorously suppressed. Cp. the following:—" Then there was *a great roar* that Mord handled the suit well, but it was said that Flosi and his men betook them only to quibbling and wrong."—[Das., u. s. and passim.]

notice has been lawfully made, as also of the fact that the nine neighbours have been duly summoned to ride to the Althing, and sit on the inquest, " to find whether Flosi, Thord's son, rushed with an assault laid down by law on Helgi, Njál's son."

§ 41. This concluded the preliminary proceedings, which, it will be seen, answered to the modern taking out a summons against a man (búa mál á hendr e-m). The suit is now said to be set on foot, "nú er mál tilbúit;" and before following it through its next stage at the Althing, we may here conveniently pause for a moment to consider the leading aspects of the procedure. "The Icelandic law-suit," to quote once more Mr. Dasent's words, "was based on the evidence of the community, supported by oath. At every step solemn witness was taken, and to fail in producing such witness was to lose the suit." In one form or another, this system of sworn witnesses seems to have been common to all the members of the Teutonic race. In Norway, as on the Continent, the same appears under a different form in the system of compurgation; and it would hardly be incorrect to assume that the *inquest by sworn recognitors* of the Frank kings, to which the English jury system is directly traceable, is only another aspect of the same principle; for "the sworn recognitors were rather witnesses than judges; they swore to facts within their own knowledge; the magistrate to whom the inquiry was entrusted was the inquirer, and he inquired through the oath of men sworn

Importance of Oaths, and of Technical Accuracy.

to speak the truth, and selected in consequence of their character and local knowledge [v]." Nor is the general principle, on which each separate yet cognate system rests, far to seek. In the semi-civilised age to which it belongs, something of the kind must have been a necessity, as the only adequate means of establishing the respectability of a man's character. But more, it answers to the modern practice of *affidavits*, and the similar machinery of the law; and in Iceland, at any rate, where writing had not yet come into general practice, the value of such a system of oath-taking and witnesses is easily conceivable.

Another equally important circumstance, which recurs at every stage of the Icelandic law-suit, is the absolute necessity of following the precise wording of the formulæ prescribed by law, of accurately repeating every technicality, and every circumstance in the exact order, and never altering a word of the notice. A single slip, or transposition of words, is sufficient to quash the proceedings. This refinement, so to speak, of technical forms has already been noticed; but a few words may be added here, to illustrate its importance. A lively and amusing instance of the fact is given in the Njála, when Gunnar, as Huckster Hedinn, guilefully summons Hrut, by making him utter the summons, and repeating it after him word for word [x]. Its importance is conspicuous in every page of the description

---

[v] Stubbs' Const. Hist., i. 612—614.
[x] Das. B. Nj., i. 70, 71.

of the suit between Mord and Flosi; for example, "the witnesses a second time bore witness of the notice before the court, and put the wounds first, and the assault last, *and used all the same words as before*[y]," &c. Again, when the actual pleading before the court begins, it is noticeable that Mord begins his case by a sort of saving clause, to secure himself against all mistakes, which he might accidentally make. "I take witness to this, that I except all mistakes in words in my pleading, whether they be too many or wrongly spoken, and *I claim the right to amend all my words, until I have put them into a proper and lawful shape*. I take witness to myself of this[z]."

§ 42. The Althing is set; the day for the declaration of the suit (mála tilskipan) is come, and men go to the Hill of Laws. Then Mord stands up, and takes witness, and gives formal notice of his suit against Flosi, declaring that "he ought to be made a guilty man, an outlaw[a] . . . and that his goods are forfeited half to me, and half to the men of the quarter, who have a right by law to take his forfeited goods[b]." After that he gives notice

The Pleading.

---

[y] Das. B. Nj., ii. 246. [z] Ib., ii. 242.

[a] Sekjan Skógarmann,—the woods and deserts being the only refuge for the outlaw.

[b] The object of this confiscation is thus explained by Mr. Dasent, clxiii. "It was no easy thing to hold the férándómr or Court of Execution at a great chief's house (as the law required), who, when outlawed, either in his presence or absence at the Thing, might gather such a band of followers around him, as to set the plaintiff and the law at defiance. The law provided against this by giving the community an interest in half of the goods for-

of the assault and wounds which the defendant had inflicted on the deceased. The courts appear not to have opened for business (dómar fara út) till another day; when, the parties having assembled in the court of the quarter to which they belonged, Mord commences the proceedings by taking witness, and bidding the several litigants to cast lots for precedence. Having himself gained the first place, he next bids Flosi listen to his oath (hlýða til eiðspialls) and to the declaration of his suit (framsaga). Then he solemnly took the oath, incumbent on every one who had to perform a public duty (lögskil) in court or parliament, as judge, pleader, neighbour, or witness, that he would perform his duty according to right and law. This done, he called severally his witnesses to the notice (lýsingar vættir), and his witnesses to the handing over of the suit (sakar töku vættir), who "came before the court, and spake, so that one uttered their witness, but both confirmed it by their common consent [c]."

feited by the outlaw, the plaintiff being entitled to the other half." At the same time, the omission on the part of the Goði to name the court of execution, rendered him liable to a sentence of lesser outlawry. Grág. i. 94. "If the priest name not the Court of Execution, and has been lawfully requested thereto, he is liable to the lesser outlawry."

[c] In every case witness was borne "over the head of John" (yfir höfði Jóni), a formula which requires a word or two of explanation. *John* for a man, and *Gudruna* for a woman, were standing names in the formularies of the Icelandic code, answering to the N. or M. of our liturgy, or to those famous fictions of English law, *John Doe and Richard Roe;* cf. Das. Nj., ii. 245, n.

The next step was for the prosecutor to bid the nine neighbours on the inquest to take their seats in the court [d], and call on the defendant to challenge the inquest (ryðja kviðin); after which he took witness that his case was complete, that he "might not be thought to have left the suit, though he go away from the court to look up proofs, or on other business."

It was now the business of the defendant to try and discover some flaw in the case for the prosecution, a task which called forth all the ingenuity of the subtle advocate. In the present instance, Eyjolf, Flosi's counsel, made various attempts to quash the trial, but without success. He first challenged and set aside several of the neighbours, whom Mord had summoned on the ground of their kinship with Mord: but it afterwards appeared that they could only be set aside, if they were kinsmen to the true plaintiff (aðili); so the neighbours, who had risen up, were bidden to sit down again. The next

for another explanation; cf. ib. clxxi. From p. cl. of the same it appears, that for the formula *John*, would be substituted in court the real name of one of the judges, who like a foreman summed up the whole proceedings, and *over whose head*, or *standing before whom*, the plaintiff had pleaded his case.

[d] The expression here used, *vestr á 'Ar-bakka* (to take their seats west on the river bank), as well as the expression, *dómar fara út* (= the courts open), shews that the courts did not, like the Lögrétta, sit on the Lögberg, which was on the eastern bank. So, too, later on in this suit, Flósi and Eyjolf lose time in trying to divide the Eastfirther's Court, while their adversaries had already anticipated them by lodging a prosecution against them in the Fifth Court, which sat on the Lögberg.

attack on the inquest was on the score of two of the number being cotters, not householders (buðsetumenn en eigi bóndi). This blow, however, was also parried, when it was proved that they owned certain property, which entitled them to sit on the inquest. A more severe blow still threatened to quash the proceedings, when four out of the nine neighbours were challenged for not being the nearest dwellers to the scene of the burning; and so confident did Eyjolf and Flosi become, that a cry arose, that now the suit for the burning was really at an end, and that the defence was better than the prosecution. But it was not to be. The law was declared to allow a bare majority to return a verdict, and though the charge against the rest could not be rebutted, it merely laid a heavy penalty on the prosecutor for each neighbour he had wrongly summoned. The case for the prosecution having proved thus unassailable, the inquest, at Mord's bidding, utter their finding; and having returned a verdict against the defendant, "again a second time, they uttered their finding against Flosi, and uttered it, first about the wounds, and last about the assault; but all their other words they uttered just as they had before uttered their finding against Flosi; and brought him in truly guilty in the suit" (baru hann sannan at sokinni[e]), their verdict being uttered twice over (in case it was given *against* the defendant),

[e] The full form of delivering the verdict was as follows; "höfum ver orðit á eitt sáttir, berum á kvið burðinu, berum hann sannan at sökinni." Nj., c. 143.

in order that the law might catch the inquest tripping if it could. Then the prosecutor takes witness, and summing up all the steps of the suit, calls upon his adversary, "or that man who has to undertake the lawful defence which he has handed over to him," to begin his defence. For hitherto the efforts of the defendant had been directed to finding flaws in the prosecution. At the same time, the prosecutor reserves to himself the same right to break down the defence by "picking holes in it," declaring that, "if any such thing arises in their lawful defence, which I need to turn into a suit against them, then I claim the right to set that suit on foot against them."

§ 43. Flosi's counsel, Eyjolf, Bolverk's son, had, by what would now-a-days be called "a bit of sharp practice," made his client, on the eve of the hearing of the case, transfer his priesthood to his brother, and attach himself as Thingman to a priest in another quarter, a step which reminds one of the manner in which Publius Clodius rendered himself eligible for the tribuneship at Rome. This being, of course, unknown to the plaintiff, the suit had been carried before the Eastfirther's Court, to which it was universally supposed Flosi belonged; whereas, he having by a trick placed himself in the Northern Quarter, the case should legally have been pleaded in the court belonging to that quarter. The mistake thence arising had rendered the plaintiff liable to prosecution in his turn for dómsafglapan, or contempt of court, and this now constituted the

The Defence.

defence. "These two men," says Eyjolf, "I take to witness that I bring forward this lawful defence, that this suit was pleaded in another Quarter Court than that in which it ought to have been pleaded, and I say that for this sake their suit has come to nought."

Having regard to the claim made by Mord at the end of the case for the prosecution, to "turn anything arising in their lawful defence into a suit against them," if need be, it excites some surprise that the fact of this move on the part of Flosi having actually been made *after* the declaration of the suit, should not have been fastened upon by the prosecution as invalidating the defence[f]. That it was in their power to do so, seems implied by the determination of Eyjolf (who was well aware of the weakness of his client's case,) not to press the point "until we have no other choice left." The prosecution, however, knew that they had a winning card to play in the bribe which Eyjolf had received, and hence probably deemed it unnecessary to go into the other matter, which, perhaps, they could never have proved. For the moment Eyjolf had triumphed, and taking witness, he forbade the judges, "by a lawful priest's veto[g]," to utter judgment in the suit.

[f] Mr. Dasent, however, p. clvii., considers that the second count of irrelevancy of witness, with which Flosi was charged before the Fifth Court, included this question of change of quarter.

[g] " Ek ver Goðalýriti dómendum at dœma sök," &c. Mr. Dasent,

§ 44. It was now a mere question of time which side should anticipate the other in bringing a new prosecution before the Fifth Court. Mord, on the one hand, had two counts against his opponent, both of which were Fifth Court matters, viz. the bribe which Eyjolf had received, and the irrelevant witness which the defendants had called. As each count involved a sentence of lesser outlawry, and the two together amounted to full outlawry, it was of the utmost consequence that Mord should, if possible, set his new suit on foot at once, so as to anticipate the prosecution for contempt of court, which was hanging over his own head. This he succeeded in doing, while Eyjolf and Flosi, unconscious of the new proceedings instituted against them in the Court of Appeal, loitered in the Quarter Court trying to divide (at véfengja[h]) the judges. When at last they arrived in the Fifth Court, it was only

The Appeal in the Fimtardómr.

here and elsewhere, translates Goðalýriti, "protest *before* the priest." But why *before*? The word means the *veto of a goði*, who "alone, by virtue of his office, could thus stop a suit, whether personally, or by one of his Thingmen; so that if any one else wished thus to stop a suit, he had first to go to his liege lord, and be authorised by him to do so;" hence " taka lýret at Goði."—Cf. Vigf. Dict., s. v. lýriti. Grágás. þingskaþ, cap. 38.

[h] The Icelandic Inquest must return an unanimous verdict. But if a minority of one or two only disputed the verdict of the majority, they were bound to yield, under a penalty for contempt of court, but might state their reasons for judging differently. But if a quorum of six out of thirty-six held a different opinion, a division was taken (*ganga til véfangs*,) and no verdict could be returned. The phrase, "leggja mál i deilð," answers to the modern parliamentary expression, " Divide on a question."

to find the new suit against them on the point of commencing.

The proceedings in the higher court were similar to those in the courts below, with this important exception, that the oaths to be sworn were of a much more solemn and binding character, and had to be attested by the oaths of two vouchers, or sannaðarmenn. "I pray God," (so runs the formula [i]) "so to help me in this light and in the next, as I shall plead this suit, as I know to be most truthful and just and lawful. I believe with all my heart that Flosi is truly guilty in this suit, if I may bring forward my proofs; and I have not brought money into this court in this suit, and I will not bring it. I have not taken money, and I will not take it, neither for a lawful nor for an unlawful end." The inquest, too, was not the same as had returned the verdict in the Quarter Court; but a new one of nine neighbours, who lived next the Thingfield.

Each step of the new suit was successfully gone through; the inquest unchallenged returned their verdict; the "foreman" of the judges summed up [k];

---

[i] " Biðek svá Goð hjálpa mer í þrisa ljósi ok í áðru (i.e. in this life and in the next) . . . . . . hefka ek fé borit í dóm þenna til liðs mer um sök þessa," &c. It does not appear to have been the practice to pay an advocate a direct fee; but after the proceedings were all over, a handsome present might be given to the successful advocate by his client. Mr. Dasent must be speaking euphemistically when he says, clv., that Flosi obtained " *by a heavy fee* the help of a great lawyer," meaning Eyjolf.

[k] This was termed "reifa málit," and the foremen appointed by

and the prosecutor taking witness, forbade the defendant to set up his defence, and prayed the judges to give the judgment. So far the case for the prosecution had been conducted with consummate skill; now, however, when there seemed no doubt about the result, a false step was made, which is as surprising as it was fatal. The Fifth Court consisted of forty-eight members; but as a certain sanctity attached to the "three twelves" from the immemorial usage, which had required that particular number to give judgment, it was enacted that no judgment of the High Court of Appeal should be valid if pronounced by more than thirty-six of its members. For this purpose the plaintiff was to call and set aside six men out of the court, and the defendant was to do the same. In case either refused to do so, the other was to call and set aside all the twelve. Mord then set aside his six; but the wary Eyjolf refused, when called upon to do so, to set aside the other six. Mord thereupon immediately made the remaining forty-two judges pass judgment in the case; a mistake which his adversary took instant advantage of, by declaring that their judgment had come to nought, "for that three twelves and one-half had judged, when three only ought to have given judgment."

§ 45. What excites our surprise in this unfortunate termination to the great trial is, that Mord should have been so ignorant of this provision of *Failure of the suit.*

plaintiff and defendant to sum up their cases were called Reifingarmenn.

the law. Or can it be supposed, when we call to mind his agreement with his father, Valgard the Guileful[1], that at the last moment he proved a traitor to the cause he had taken in hand? This conclusion seems to be something more than mere conjecture, when it is recollected that it was through the machinations of these two men that the murder of Hauskuld, priest of Whiteness, was brought about, which led to all the subsequent disasters[m]; that it was only by dint of threats that Mord could be prevailed upon to undertake the pleading[n]; and lastly, that he had only just been warned by Gizur the White not to take this false step, when he actually did so.

The point, however, which it specially serves to illustrate, is the fatal elevation of the *letter* above the *spirit* of the law in Iceland, a defect which rendered null and void even the solemn and unanimous decision of the High Court of Appeal. For, here was a case, in which the guilt of the defendant had been so irrefutably proved, that he had not even been able to set up a defence, and in which an unanimous judgment had actually been passed, suddenly brought to nought, because that judgment had been endorsed by six judges more than were by law required! Truly, if the Icelandic law did shew a commendable good sense in providing that the recalcitrant obstinacy of a small minority should not hinder the passing of judgment, it shewed no

---

[1] B. Nj., ii. 101, 102.   [m] Ib., pp. 101—103.
[n] Ib., pp. 208, 209.

less a deplorable folly in allowing a mere quibble and quirk of law to override the solemn decision of the highest court in the country °.

§ 46. Before leaving the subject of legal pro- *Origin of the jury-system discussed.* cedure in Iceland, it may be expected that some reference should be made to the relations in which the modern jury-system stands to the old Icelandic kviðr. But within the limits of an essay, which cannot hope to present more than the merest outline of Icelandic institutions, and in which necessarily many of the details must be either entirely omitted, or at most only hinted at, it were impossible to enter at any length into the vexed question as to the origin of the English jury-system. When scholars like Professor Stubbs and Mr. Freeman in England, and Dr. Maurer in Germany, not to mention a host of other writers, have so fully and ably treated the question in all its bearings, but little remains to be said; nor would it be possible to do more than recapitulate the conclusions to which their indefatigable researches have led them. Still, as complete unanimity does not prevail among some of the most prominent writers on this subject, it may not be out of place to state as briefly as possible some of the leading views which are held,

---

° The last step in a trial was the holding of the féransdómr, or Court of Execution, at the outlaw's own abode within fourteen days, *aptir vápnatak*. This step was necessary to condemn a man to full outlawry, skógmaðr. The lesser outlaw, fjörbaugsmaðr could escape full outlawry by paying the fjörbaugr, or lifemoney, a fee of one mark to the féransdómr. For the latter, cf. § 42, n. b.

and endeavour to estimate, from the point of view adopted in the present essay, which of those views are most in accordance with the opinions therein set forth. This is the more necessary, because these pages aim at shewing the importance of Iceland, not only as being an unique specimen, so to speak, of one form of feudal development, but also as the forerunner of those races which now enjoy the greatest political freedom in the world, and as containing, no less than the Teutonic races of the Continent, the germs of institutions which have since flourished and become the strongest bulwarks against despotism, whether in the form of royal prerogative, or of priestly sacerdotalism.

In the first place, it is scarcely necessary to point out that to whatever origin the English jury may be traced, its development on English soil has been such as entirely to change its original character, so that the jury-system, *as at present existing*, cannot but be regarded as a purely English growth, and that too of no distant date[p]. The proof of this is sufficiently evident in the fact, that in all the original elements from which the development of this system may fairly be traced—whether compurgators, recognitors, or the sworn witnesses of the laws of Æthelstan and Eadgar,—the principle holds that they are "not judges but witnesses, witnesses declaring their verdict from their personal knowledge; while it is the essence of the modern jury that they should not use their personal knowledge,

[p] Cp. Freem. N. Conq., v. p. 452.

but should give their verdict according to the evidence laid before them by others [q]."

It may therefore be safely assumed that the jury is an English growth, developed out of various elements, some existing in the country, some introduced at various times from different external sources. In the latter case, it would doubtless be probable that one form should exercise a stronger and more lasting influence than the others; and this in truth we find to have been the case. Reduced to its earliest and simplest elements, jury trial may be described as "any kind of trial in which the case is decided by the oaths of men taken from among the community at large [r]," and as such the primitive germs of the system are "as old as any institution of the Teutonic race." Hence it is not surprising if we should find these common germs wafted to our shores by the same winds, which at different periods swept over the country the waves of Anglo-Saxon, Danish, and Norman invasion; and that the latest and most complete of those invasions, the Norman Conquest, should have moulded with a fresh element, introduced by the conquerors, many of the elements found already existing in the country; but in such wise, that this latest element should become the predominant one in the form of trial which was gradually evolved.

This fresh element is described by Professor Stubbs as the "system of recognition by sworn inquest, directly derived from the Frank capitularies, into

[q] Cp. Freem. N. Conq., v. p. 452.   [r] Ib., u. s.

which it may have been adopted from the fiscal regulations of the Theodosian code. This was the instrument which, introduced in its rough simplicity at the Conquest, was developed by the lawyers of the Plantagenet period into the modern trial by jury[s]." But even so, it cannot be described as a wholly stranger element. The Norman or Carolingian institution had its root in the same primitive ideas as the kindred old English institutions[t]." Hence it is not incorrect, nor inconsistent with the view adopted by Professor Stubbs[u], to say with Mr. Freeman that the jury is an institution which grew up gradually *out of germs common to England with other Teutonic lands;* and that " The recognitors are only another form of the same principle, which shews itself in the compurgators, in the Frithborh, in every detail of the action of popular courts [x]." What those germs were in Iceland the foregoing pages will have sufficed to shew: an attempt was there made to trace them to certain fundamental principles in the Scandinavian character; and we shall presently have occasion to recur to the subject, so far as to institute a comparison between certain details of English and Icelandic law.

But the above conclusion does not meet with uni-

---

[s] Stubbs, C. H., i. 612, 613; Cp. p. 441.   [t] Freeman.

[u] Professor Stubbs, however, seems hardly to recognise the northern element. Yet the inquest introduced by the Northmen into Normandy (where it retained its footing long after the jury-system had died out in the rest of France,) must surely have exerted a considerable influence on the form in which the institution was introduced into England.   [x] Freeman.

versal acceptance. Dr. Maurer approaches this view when he "argues for a common *North* German origin, from which the principle of jury has been developed in different ways by the several races in which it is found ʸ," and that it first made its appearance in English law along with the Normans after the Conquest. But Mr. Dasent, with M. Worsaae ᶻ, who writes as a Dane, and pleads energetically in behalf of the Danish influence in England, argues that "The trial by jury is due, in great part, to the northern influence in the Danelagh, or Scandinavian portion of England, which, at the time of the Conquest, may be roughly reckoned at half the kingdom." And he concludes that it was *not* introduced from Normandy, because "the form of trial prevalent in that country was not, as in Iceland, trial by jury, but that by compurgation ᵃ. . . . which was common in Norway, as well as in all the Teutonic races. Thus it existed in England among the Anglo-Saxons, and it came from Norway into Normandy along with the followers of Rollo, and thence it went with them into England ᵇ." And Mr. Vigfússon (s. v. Kviðr) says, "From the analogy of Icelandic customs it can be inferred with

---

ʸ Stubbs, C. II., i. p. 612, n. 1.   ᶻ Cf. Worsaae, "The Danes in England."

ᵃ In the Norse law, a man was discharged upon the joint oath of himself and a certain number of men—Compurgators. In the Icelandic Commonwealth these are scarcely mentioned, the kviðr taking their place (cp. Sir E. Head, Glum, p. 119); but after the union with Norway the Norse procedure was partly introduced into Iceland.—Vigf., s. v. eiðr.   ᵇ Introd. to Vigf.

certainty, that along with the invasion of the Danes and Northmen, the judgment by verdict was also transplanted to England. For the settlers in England were kith and kin to those of Iceland, carrying with them the same laws and customs. After the Conquest, it became the law of the land."

<small>Comparison between Icelandic and Anglo-Saxon Courts.</small>

§ 47. The conclusion here arrived at, manifestly attributes too much importance to Danish influence in the presence of the Norman Conquest. It can hardly be asserted with accuracy, that the Normans assumed from their conquered subjects the most important of their judicial institutions, or that the system of recognitors, which can be proved to have been introduced at the time of the Conquest, should have wholly succumbed to the paramount influence of Danish law and custom. But, on the other hand, it may with reason be contended, that to attribute the origin of the jury-system solely to the introduction by the Normans of the system of recognitors, would be to err in the opposite direction. For the aim of the Conqueror's policy was the " maintenance of *the local and provincial machinery of the English system* with the central and sovereign authority characteristic of the Norman [c]." To enter into any details of that machinery would be foreign to our present purpose. But the following description of the Anglo-Saxon Courts of Justice, by one of the leading jurists of the day, is worth quoting, not only on account of the close resemblance which it bears to

[c] Stubbs, C. H., i. p. 436.

the constitution and action of the Icelandic courts, but also as illustrating the early predominance in our own institutions of the same spirit of self-government to which the Icelandic kviðr owed its origin. "A criminal trial[d]," writes Sir J. F. Stephen, "must have been a kind of public meeting, presided over by officers, the bishop and sheriff, who saw that certain forms which left them no discretion were complied with, and who carried out the consequences which legally resulted from the enquiry. The institution of the proceedings, and the collection of the evidence, by which each side supported its own case, was entirely under the control of accusers and accused. The Judges had nothing to do with the matter . . . . the whole proceedings were essentially free and local; and the system left almost unlimited discretion in the hands of persons locally interested, and especially in those of the party injured." In its general outline, the above description closely corresponds to the chief features of the Icelandic courts. Such similarity, however, proves, not that the latter are the origin of the English courts, but rather that both find a common origin in the fundamental principle of the Teutonic character already noticed. And thus we have one proof the more of the essentially Teutonic nature of English character and English institutions, and of the persistence of the Teutonic element in our national life, in the face of all other influences. Its importance, too, in secur-

---

[d] Criminal Law, p. 14.

ing the liberties of the people, is inestimable. It is through the assizes alone, as Lord Brougham remarked, that the mass of the people can take part in the administration of justice, under the auspices of the superior judges of the realm; and it is by such taking part in, and personally witnessing the administration of justice, that the nation places such confidence in it; and that the harshness of the penal code has been gradually softened, so as to bring it into harmony, in its spirit and temper, with the mind and character of the whole nation.

Nature of Northern influence in England.

§ 48. The influence of the Danes in England has been much exaggerated by those who seek in every detail of the English organisation traces of the Northman's occupation. "The views of northern antiquaries, who refer every point of similarity between Scandinavia and England to Norse and Danish influences in Britain, seem to be maintained in ignorance of the body of English History, which existed earlier than the Norse invasions, the civilising and Christianising influence of England on Scandinavia, and the common stock of institutions that both nationalities possessed[e]." Nor was the duration of Danish supremacy in Britain as long as some writers have unhesitatingly averred. Mr. Laing, in speaking of the "laws and usages of the Northmen as prevailing over a large part of the island for nearly 300 years[f]," forgets that, although England had, before the Conquest by Swegen in

---

[e] Stubbs, C. H., i. 203, n. 1.   [f] Kings of Norway, i. p. 105.

1013, been largely ravaged and even partly occupied, yet these ravages were, as Mr. Freeman points out, "in their own nature temporary, and the Danes, who had settled in England, had been gradually brought into a greater or less degree of submission to the English king, into a greater or less degree of amalgamation with the English people [g];" and that it was not till as late as 1017 that the Danish Cnut could claim an undivided sovereignty over the whole country [h]. But short as was the period of the Danish supremacy, the benefits they conferred were lasting, and are to be found in the new ideas introduced, or, more correctly, in the resuscitation of old ideas, which were then dying out; in the fresh spirit of independence, which their presence infused into the flagging energies of the Saxons, and the consolidation of the kingdom forced upon the latter, by being compelled to combine against a common foe [i]. The Danes were English-

[g] Norm. Conq., i. 361.

[h] Till the days of Swegen and Cnut, the boundary of the Danish conquests seems to have been the same as that marked by the treaty between Ælfred and Guthrum, viz., "Upon the Thames, along the Lea to its source, then right to Bedford, and then upon the Ouse to Watling Street." The survival of such territorial divisions as the *Rapes* [Hreppar] of Bramber, in Sussex, indicates perhaps the extent of their influence southwards; and in the Laws of Edgar we find "a distinct recognition of the right of the Danes of the Danelaga, not only to retain their own customs, but to modify them on occasion."—Stubbs, C. H., i.

[i] Cp. M. Bonnechose, Hist. d'Anglet., i. 148, who also remarks, that the Danish invasions necessitated the building of many fortresses, which eventually became walled towns defended by warlike populations.—Cp. Freeman, Norm. Conq., i. 52—54.

men no less than those whom they were conquering; but they were Englishmen in a less advanced stage of culture, and consequently of a freer, rougher type, just as the Normans were Danes, who had become Frenchmen. This community of race explains the persistence throughout English History of the same ideas, customs and institutions. Danes and Normans alike contributed, not to sweep away, but to intensify and add to the development of the existing organisation. This fact, the kinship between the conquering and the conquered races, supplies the link of the chain connecting England with Iceland. The Danes who ravaged, and settled on, the coasts of England, and the Northmen who settled in Gaul, and adopted the exterior and superficial characteristics of Frenchmen, were the same race of men as the settlers of Iceland. Hence it was inevitable that common ideas, common feelings, and common traditions should transmit themselves, and become part of the inheritance of those with whom they mixed. Hence the truth of what has already been stated, that the Viking spirit of the Northmen has entered into the English character, and has been instrumental in saving England alike from the curse of a feudal nobility, and the oppression of a tyrannical absolutism.

PART III.

INTRODUCTION OF CHRISTIANITY AND FALL OF REPUBLIC.

§ 49. THE consideration of the Icelandic Church, and its relations with the temporal power of the State, most properly belongs to the period of history dealing with the Fall of the Republic. For Christianity was not established in the island till the year 1000 A.D., four years before the erection of the Fifth Court, and could thus in nowise affect the development of the Constitution; whereas it did contribute very materially to the subversion of Icelandic independence. It would be beyond the scope of the present essay to dwell upon the details of Church organisation and administration in Iceland. However interesting the inquiry, it must suffice to refer for all questions of internal administration, to the elaborate work of Dr. Maurer, who has brought together all the information available on this subject[a]. Our present object is rather to note how, after the establishment of Christianity in Iceland, the Church rapidly grew in power, till it became the rival of the state, and engaged with it in those deadly feuds, which more than anything else contributed to the decay of freedom in the island.

General Sketch.

[a] Isl., 220—278.

But the Church was not the sole cause of the final overthrow of the Icelandic Commonwealth. The very principle of individual liberty, which it had been ever the pride of the Norseman to maintain, itself contributed in no small degree to the destruction of the nation's freedom. Uncontrolled by any powerful central authority, the great independent chiefs of the land were constantly embroiled in internecine feuds, which not only wasted the strength of the nation, but even called for foreign interference, and thus paved the way to their final subjection to the throne of Norway.

Co-operating with these internal causes, was the external pressure brought to bear upon the island, by the repeated attempts made by successive kings of Norway to bring it under their control. The union with Norway has been termed subjection to the throne of Norway; and this expression is justified by much of the later history of the island. Professor Maurer also says, that in 1264, "Der Isländische Freistaat war in der That zu einem Norwegischen Schatzlande geworden [b]." At the same time, it is but just to observe that the instrument by which this political connexion was sealed, was really an act of union, which bore all the marks of independent voluntariness which might be expected from the character of the nation. Particular care was taken that this union should not take the form of political subjection to another nation; as is sufficiently testified by the following words, with

[b] Isl., p. 138.

which the Act of Union concludes:—"We and our heirs will observe fidelity towards you, so long as you and your heirs keep your promises to us, and adhere to the above-named resolutions; but we declare ourselves to be released from our engagements if, in the opinion of the most honourable men, you break faith with us." Hence Professor Münch has grounds for remarking, that "Iceland was united to Norway, without becoming an actual province of it; and neither in an administrative respect could it be accounted so."

§ 50. It was in the closing summer of the tenth century that the first tidings of the change of faith in Norway, under Olaf Tryggveson reached Iceland, and presently Thangbrand arrived, "who taught the people Christianity, and baptised all who took the faith [c]." But Thangbrand had too little of the priest about him to effect much; the people resisted the subversion of their religious principles; and so, "after passing a winter or two in the island, and slaying two or three men who had insulted him, he returned to Norway," and assured King Olaf that it was a hopeless task to try and convert Iceland. But volunteers were found to undertake the work; and the next summer they sailed out to Iceland in time for the meeting of the Althing, and summoning all the friends of the new faith, rode armed to the parliament. There they nearly came to blows with the opposite party, who had also mus-

Christianity introduced by Law.

[c] Isl., c. 7.

tered an armed force. The next day the leaders of the Christian party stood forth on the Lögberg, and declared their business in such wise as to excite universal admiration [d]. But though they got a hearing, they could not convince the assembly, and with all due solemnity, each declared the other outside the community, and withdrew from the Hill of Laws. In these straits men had recourse to the Speaker of the Law, and urged him to solve the difficulty of the position [e]. He withdrew, and remained apart the whole day and the succeeding night in deep thought, without speaking a word. The next morning he arose, and assembling the people at the Hill of Laws, brought forward proposals for restoring peace to the community. In a speech of studied moderation, he urged upon both parties the ruin which their division would bring upon the country, and the consequent necessity of striking a compromise acceptable to both. He proposed, therefore, that the whole people should be baptised and profess Christianity; that all temples and images of the heathen gods might be destroyed with impunity; that the public worship of the old gods might, on conviction, be punished by banishment; but no one should be punished for

[d] Islend., c. 7.

[e] It appears that he received three marks for the part he took in the matter. 'This, says Mr. Dasent, was his proper fee; the word, however, in the original, *ceypti*, implies a direct bribe. Dr. Maurer supports this view, as he speaks of bribery in connexion with the matter, (Isl., 82); and Dahlmann takes *ceypti*, (erkaufte) = bribed.

privately sacrificing to them [f]. On the other hand, the heathen practices of exposing children and of eating horse-flesh, were to be retained. These proposals, however unpalatable to the heathen party, who thought they had been betrayed [g], were loyally acquiesced in by both parties, a fact which, considering the excited state of public feeling at the time, speaks volumes for the good sense of the people, and shews how deeply seated already in the Icelandic character was that constitutional love of law and order, which, at the present day also, forms the distinguishing characteristic of their latest descendants, the American people. The retention of certain old heathen practices was perhaps dictated as much by motives of economy, as out of deference to popular prejudices [h]. But the prohibition of all inquisitorial interference with the private religion of the individual is highly characteristic of the religious feelings of the Northmen, which allowed "every man to be his own priest," and contrasts forcibly with the tyranny and bigotry of later ages, even in our own country. England may well feel shame and remorse for her Oxford and Smithfield *auto-da-fés;* but Iceland cannot boast of a single martyr.

§ 51. It is curious to trace in the development of the religion thus introduced, and which slowly but surely took firm root in the national affections, the

The Church advances towards

[f] Isl., c. 7; cf. App. F.
[g] "þóttuz heiðnir menn miok sviknir vera." Nj., c. 106.
[h] Cf. Mau. Isl., p. 81.

I

the acquisition of temporal power.

working of those principles of individualism and self-government, out of which we have seen the Icelandic Commonwealth arise. Just as in the early days of the Landnám-tide, every one who chose, or had power to do so, built himself a temple, so now the building of Christian churches was left entirely to private energy and zeal. None were compelled to contribute to their erection, though no doubt much moral pressure was brought to bear upon individual liberality by the hopes and fears of a future existence held out by the clergy. For instance, a curious legend occurs in the Eyrbyggia S., c. 49, that a man could grant as many souls a seat in heaven, as the church which he built held persons. As the establishment was voluntary, so also was the endowment. At first, no doubt many of the founders of churches took orders and conducted their own services; otherwise they had to hire a priest, as they would any other servant. Later, when Bishop Gizor founded the first bishopric of Iceland, he made regular provision for it by endowing it with lands; and by the instrumentality of the same Bishop tithes were introduced by law, an endowment which in course of time rendered the clergy to a certain degree independent of their patrons. That the payment of tithes was a purely voluntary act on the part of the people is insisted on by the author of the Islendingabók, c. 10, who describes how, out of affection and devotion to their beloved bishop, all men resolved to have their goods valued, and pay tithes to the Church. Beyond this, the State did no more than accord to the Church a certain kirkjuhelgi (or inviolability), as before it had granted the hofshelgi to the temple system. State-Church, in the modern sense of the term, there was none. On the other hand, the Church was essentially national, for the bishops were elected by the people in their assemblies, and instead of a bare majority of the people, the whole nation acknowledged a common Church. The appointment of priests was entirely in the hands of the patrons, though it was in the power of the bishops to refuse to admit to Holy Orders those whom they deemed improper persons. Thus, while not unfrequently wealthy chiefs of powerful houses were to be found in the ranks of the clergy, on the other hand, persons of mean birth and low education were often hired as chaplains[1]. These circumstances, combined with the absence of celibacy among the clergy, gave them a semi-lay and eminently national character, which, however beneficial (as it proved) to the development of a national literature, contributed to lower the standard of education, and to introduce a general worldliness of feeling.

§ 52. The bishops occupied seats in the Lögretta, and possessed no doubt the influence due to their position and superior education, but all ecclesiastical legislation was in the hands of the Althing; and at first, at least, there was no question of a separate spiritual jurisdiction, as neither were the clergy

Questions of Supremacy, &c., lead to disputes between Church and State.

---

[1] For all the churches were, in Norse phrase, hœgindiskirkjur, or private chapels,—as opposed to heraðskirkjur.

exempted from temporal burdens or secular duties.
Nor, so long as the diocese of Iceland was subject to
the Metropolitan of Denmark, was there any danger
of such questions being raised as were likely to lead
to a collision between Church and State. The
Danish Metropolitan had enough to think of, without troubling himself much with the internal affairs
of the distant island. But the erection of a Metropolitan Church in Norway wrought a great change.
It brought Iceland into far closer union than before
with the rest of the Western Church, at a moment
when a more uninterrupted intercourse with other
lands was inspiring the Norse Church with the reforming energy of Gregory VII. Henceforth, the
Icelandic clergy began to feel themselves to be an
integral portion of the universal hierarchy of the
Western Church. An era of reform, and of stricter
Church discipline was inaugurated, and the Church
at once advanced along that path of independence,
which was ere long to lead to open conflict with the
secular authority of the country.

The suspension of the clergy guilty of manslaughter and other crimes, the attempt to put
a stop to the warlike dispositions which the carrying of arms engendered, and the prohibition to
undertake the law-suits of others[k], or otherwise in-

[k] This prohibition is, as Dr. Maurer points out, the more strange, because the then Bishop of Skálholt was one of the most skilful lawyers of the day. Perhaps the dictum of William of Malmesbury respecting the English clergy after the Norman Conquest, "nullus clericus nisi causidicus," was equally applicable to the Icelandic clergy.

terfere in secular affairs, were necessary measures, demanded by the hitherto lax discipline of the Church, and the closer attention which her increasing cares required of her sons. Nor, from this point of view, was the prohibition against the possession of Goðorðs by the clergy objectionable [1], though by tending to their accumulation in fewer hands, the political effect was to widen the growing breach between the spiritual and temporal powers of the State. But the reformers, who instituted these changes, by degrees grew into a hierarchical sect, whose principles tended to asceticism and sacerdotalism, and whose aim was the severance of Church from State. Under these circumstances, a fitting occasion only was required to bring about that open collision, to which the altered relations of the two parties in the State had inevitably led. That occasion was not far to seek. Questions raised by the canonization of saints soon led to bitter conflicts, in the course of which the extreme party appealed to the Metropolitan of Norway, and even to the Pope, who gladly availed himself of so favourable an opportunity of interfering in the affairs of the island. But the blindness of the hierarchical party had led them to throw away their real independence in the vain pursuit of a shadow; and the interference of foreign powers, which they had courted, resulted in the appointment of foreign

[1] In spite of this prohibition, the clergy seem to have retained their Goðorðs till the union with Norway. Cf. Schlegel's Introduction to Grágás, p. xvi.

bishops, without either native clergy or laity having a voice in the matter; while the Norse kings were not slow to seize the additional hold thus proffered to them on the country they coveted.

It is remarkable that, just as the introduction of Christianity led to events which brought about the fall of the Republic, so, in their later history, the Icelanders "look upon the introduction of the Reformation as the greatest misfortune that could have befallen them [m]," for it did away with the only counterpoise to kingly authority which then existed in the country, dispersed its wealth by the suppression of the Roman Catholic priesthood, and destroyed the education of the people, which was in the hands of the clergy.

Even at this late date, the history of the Icelandic Church is not without interest as a warning example. It is not difficult to-day to trace in the struggles of Ultramontanes on the Continent and Ritualists in England, those same tactics, which, in Iceland, led to the overthrow first, of ecclesiastical, and next, of national independence.

<small>Defects of the Goðorð system.</small> § 53. But whilst the clerical party in the State was thus gravitating towards Norwegian influence and interference, other forces were at work, which gradually undermined the whole Goðorð organisation of the country—the pillar, as Dr. Maurer calls it [n], which supported the constitution,—and threatened to resolve the whole back into the dis-

[m] Prof. Paijkull.   [n] Isl., p. 99.

integrated elements from which it had sprung. These forces were simply the natural outworking of those defects, which, from the first, had been inherent in the political system of the country. But those defects were aggravated, and their evil results hastened, partly by the effect, and partly by the failure, of those reforms on which the salvation of the Commonwealth had once seemed to depend.

The Goðorð system was, as has been already seen, unique. The Goði possessed all the attributes of the Teutonic Kinglet, but, owing to the peculiar conditions of Iceland, far more real power. Again, the Goðorð was an inheritance, and as such might be handed down from father to son; but unlike the old Norse oðal, which was inalienable, it might be bought and sold, split up into lots, or even held in partnership; thus answering much more to personalty, than to realty. Further, the relationship between the Goði and his Thingman was based upon a purely personal agreement, which was liable at any moment to be dissolved. From these circumstances there resulted a tendency, on the one hand, to infinite divisibility, and on the other, to the aggregation of separate and distinct Goðorðs into the hands of single chiefs. This double tendency was increased by the collapse of the Quarter-thing system. It has already been shewn how the use of the Quarter-things was very soon superseded by the Var-things and the Quarter Courts at the Althing. How completely they fell into disuse is proved by the fact that they are scarcely ever mentioned, and then only as belonging to the west quarter[o].

The natural consequence of such absence of local parliaments was, to destroy the independence of the people; disuse rendering them negligent of their own interests, and incapable of directing their own affairs. The process of disintegration thus commenced, was increased by the perversion of the local organisation, which had substituted the samþingi, or union of three Goðar, for the independent jurisdiction of individual priests. The law, indeed, required that the samþingisgoðar should hold their spring and autumn meetings regularly at a certain fixed spot; but at the same time exceptions were permitted, by which not only were the places of meeting shifted, but the unions themselves might be broken up, or fresh ones formed by the combination of several existing ones. Further, the numerous new Goðorðs, which the erection of the Fifth Court necessitated, produced a like departure from the old system, which was attended with similar results. For the owners of these Goðorðs, external as it were to the political organisation of the country, were at the same time secure of even greater independence than belonged to the old established Goðar. They could hold their own meetings at places of their own selection; and the advantages which such freedom offered induced, no doubt, many of the samþingisgoðar to separate themselves unlawfully from their own districts.

[o] M. Isl., p. 100.

§ 54. Thus was gradually destroyed that balance of power between the various semi-independent chiefs, on which, in the absence of any compensating supreme authority, the safety of the Republic depended. One chief after another gradually acquired a preponderating influence over his fellows, either by the greater number of Thingmen who acknowledged his lordship, or by the increased territorial influence which the acquisition of numerous Goðorðs, and his extensive connexions with other chiefs, had placed in his hands. This centralisation not only brought about a radical change in the character of the Goðorð, but also altered the hitherto existing relations between Goði and Thingman. Instead of a purely personal, wholly undefined influence, controlling men, it may be, in every part of the island, the Goði now assumes a territorial sway over clearly-defined geographical districts. New names are adopted, and old ones used in a new sense. Thus takmörk now, for the first time, is applied to the ancient þingsókn and þingmark, while these also have lost their former signification. So, too, as the Goðar rise to the haughty position of territorial lords, their Thingmen sink to the level of dependent subjects. The privilege belonging to the Thingman, of leaving his þingsókn and attaching himself to a new Goði, if ever it had been put into practice, became now utterly impracticable. The nobles, having acquired the reality, soon adopted the symbols of a power which was feudal all but in name, and marched about at the head of armed

Internal disturbances and general disorder.

bands, with banners flying, and displaying all the pomp of military power. Hence, not unnaturally, the idea would present itself to the most powerful chieftain of some district to obtain, by a *coup d'état*, the sovereignty over his own division, or even over the whole island. Jealousies and feuds arose, which resulted in the open wars of the Sturlung age, during which the history of Iceland, as formerly that of the Roman Empire, was reduced to a chronicle of the private quarrels of individual opponents. These wars completed the disintegration of the State. The *solidarité* which identity of interests promotes, was gone, when those interests were no longer identical but antagonistic; the cohesion, which the habits of working together in the Althing and the Samþingi had promoted, disappeared, as soon as the only bonds which held the several elements together were loosened. And in the place of a well co-ordinated system, of members thoroughly harmonised and working together in peaceful order, there remained the disturbed spectacle of warring elements engaged in the work of mutual destruction.

Union of Iceland with Norway.

§ 55. Under these circumstances, it may excite surprise that the fall of the Republic was not followed by a military despotism. Had Iceland been entirely left to itself, this can hardly have failed to have been the case. But the effect of the introduction of Christianity had been, to bring the Commonwealth into a closer relation with Norway than ever before, and this relation became developed into absolute subjection by circumstances to which we must now briefly refer. From very early times the kings' of Norway had endeavoured to impose taxation upon the Icelanders; but the strenuous opposition of the latter, and the troubles with which the kings had to contend at home, had constantly frustrated their attempts; so that, far on in the twelfth century, the Icelanders could still boast, in the words of the German historian, "*Apud illos non est rex, nisi tantum lex*[p]." But, though they thus steadily refused the yoke of tribute, it had early been the custom for young Icelanders to offer their services to the Norwegian sovereigns, as well as to other foreign jarls or kings; and it was while serving under these that they penetrated other lands, even to distant Micklegarth (Constantinople), where, under the title of Varangians, they acquired a well-earned fame. Indeed, though perhaps most students of Greek history are ignorant of the fact, the Piræus itself was captured " by no less a person than King Harold Harðraða, who, before he mounted the throne of Norway, was captain of the Varangians at Constantinople." This fact is recorded in Runic characters on a colossal lion, which was carried off by the Venetians in 1687 from the Piræus to Venice, where it now stands at the entrance to the Arsenal [q]. Though many would thus fight and die abroad, and some make Norway their permanent home, many more must have returned to Iceland, thus forming the nucleus of a king's party,

[p] Ad. Bremen, 385.   [q] Das. Nj., ii. 499.

which, in the subsequent complications, when patriotism was swallowed up by party spirit, must have stood the Norse kings in good stead. Indeed, the manner in which King Hakon deals with the most powerful chieftains, even in the earlier stages of these struggles, summoning them to Norway, and detaining them there or sending them back at pleasure, proves most clearly that the allegiance once taken upon themselves by the Icelandic nobles was never cast off, but that it was even looked upon by them as an honour. On the other hand, the authority which he already early assumed over parts of the island, treating them no otherwise than he would his own Norway, demands a somewhat different explanation; which is found in the fact that, in many cases, the territorial lordships were actually ceded by their owners to the king, in return, it may be, for other more valued possessions, or even a promotion to some higher title. Thus the old right of alienating Goðorðs was abused to the detriment of the country, partly in consequence of the malpractice, as Maurer calls it[r], of taking foreign service, and partly from the eagerness of the warring factions to secure, at any price, the support of the king against their rivals[s].

---

[r] Island., p. 140.

[s] The subsequent history of Iceland, after its union with Norway, does not come within the scope of this Essay; for an interesting account of the later vicissitudes of the island, and its present relations with Denmark, it is sufficient to refer to the work of Professor Paijkull, already quoted.

§ 56. The closing scenes of the dying Republic are sad to contemplate. The spectacle of men, once fired with the proud spirit of independence, and scorning to acknowledge a master's authority, now so blinded by the passions of religious strife and party feuds, as to vie with one another in cringing before the monarchs whose attacks they had for ages resisted; this betrays the moral change which had passed over the nation since the day when Ingólfr Arnarson[t] first set foot upon the island.

Criticism of the Icelandic Constitution.

And yet this is not the least instructive portion of Icelandic history, for it suggests some points for criticism as to the nature of the Icelandic Constitution, and, more generally, illustrates the origin of the worst evils to which some forms of government are liable. The radical defect of the Icelandic Constitution was the absence of any sufficient force in the hands of the supreme authority of the State. The preceding examination of the growth of the Commonwealth suffices to shew, that the political organisation of Iceland was throughout of a local and not of a central character. The Althing was merely an annual meeting of the separate heads of the local administration for the transaction of common business. As it lasted but fourteen days, the whole administration of the country, during by far the greatest part of the year, was carried on in the several districts under the heraðsstjorn of the various samþingisgoðar; the central government, as represented by their landsstjorn, being in abey-

[t] He was the first settler. Islendingabók, c. 6.

ance. Aristocratic in character from the first, it assumed more and more, as time went on, the nature of a close oligarchy. Fearful of entrusting too much authority to anyone save themselves, the ruling chiefs so limited and hedged around the lawfully-constituted supreme authority of the State (in the person of the Lögsögumaðr) that he had absolutely no force at his disposal for quelling any disturbances, or breach of the peace that might occur[a]. More care was taken to check any undue excess of his powers, and punish any neglect of his duty, than to provide him with the force necessary for maintaining his authority, and the dignity of the State. Police there was none. Law was the sole ruling power acknowledged by these proud, independent chiefs; of whom, as of the ancient Greeks, it might be said that νόμος ὁ βασίλευς. But they failed to see that law, without a sufficient sanction in the shape of material force to back it up, is apt to degenerate into lawlessness and anarchy. And such, in fact, was the inevitable consequence. It was impossible to prevent fights arising between contending factions or rival chiefs, and often the one party would by force prevent their opponents from obtaining a fair hearing in open court. Numerous instances occur of local Things being in consequence abolished, and, as noticed above, this was the cause of the decay of the old private courts of justice. But even the Althing itself was liable

---

[a] Maurer, Isl., p. 219. "Von allen Befügnissen welche irgendwie mit der Executivgewalt zusammenhiengen, war er aufs Sorgfältigste ausgeschlossen."

to have its session thus abruptly terminated, as the great battle at the Althing, consequent on the failure of the suit between Mord and Flosi, shews. And once, in 1238, no Althing was held at all, in consequence of civil disturbances. All this goes to prove that the Icelandic Constitution was by no means so simple as at first sight might appear. It was, on the contrary, a most delicately arranged organisation. The stability and order of the country depended upon the balance of power between the several Goðar being carefully poised, so that none should gain an excessive superiority over the others. As soon as that balance of power was upset by the accumulation of Goðorðs in the hands of single chiefs, the sole restraining force which had maintained peace and order was gone; anarchy and oppression of a necessity intervened, and the strong arm of the Norwegian monarch providentially restored order when the country was trembling on the brink of a military despotism.

§ 57. In a constitutional government, be the head of the State, emperor, king, or president, the two chambers and the sovereign re-act upon each other as checks, so that any undue exercise of the powers belonging to each is, in a great measure at least, prevented. In Iceland there was no idea of a second chamber. This absence of the germs of what we call constitutional government, was not owing to the conditions under which the settlement of Iceland took place. Rather it is noticeable, that in the early organisation of Norway itself, no trace

The Polity of Scandinavia different from that of the Southern Teutons. Parallel between Iceland and England.

appears of those elements which are dwelt upon by Tacitus as existing among the Teutons of the mainland. While the social system is common to both branches, the political organisation of the Northern, or Scandinavian branch, is decidedly less advanced than that of the Southern. In both we have the open assemblies, in which every freeman has a right to take part; in both we have kings acting as chief magistrates, and possessed of a limited authority. But there is nothing in the Scandinavian branch answering to the *principes*, or "official magistracy," who transacted the details of public business without consulting the mass of the people; or the *comitatus*, or "body of warlike companions who attached themselves in the closest manner to the chieftain of their choice[x]." The reasons of this difference it behoves us not to inquire into now; it is sufficient to hint at the fact that the Teutons, who encroached upon and invaded the Roman empire, were necessarily subjected to different conditions from their brethren who peopled Scandinavia. In the former case, they were warriors planting themselves in a country already occupied; in the latter, they were settlers spreading themselves over an empty territory[y]. But its importance is not in-

[x] Stubbs, Const. Hist., i. 24.

[y] A comparison between the contemporaneous settlement of Iceland and the conquest of Normandy, goes far to confirm this view. In the former case, each held his land by oðal right; in the latter, the same race coming into a country already peopled, which they had to conquer from the former owners, naturally adopted the feudal social arrangement.

considerable; and, in relation to the later history of Iceland and England, is of great interest. For, in the former country, we see the most perfect and unhindered development of the one system, while in the latter we have almost as perfect, because also unhindered, a development of the other. Iceland, owing to its position, was in a manner outside the political system of Europe. Norway was unable to secure any ascendancy in the island till the Republic was on the point of falling. Even Christianity gained no footing there till its constitution was complete. Hence we have in Iceland a perfect pattern of the ancient Scandinavian polity in its fullest development, as it had grown up spontaneously and in uninterrupted isolation. In England, on the other hand, we have an example of the legitimate development of the semi-feudal polity belonging to the Teutonic nations of the Continent, which has grown up spontaneously, protected from the rougher gales which have passed over the Continent by the favouring influence of England's insular position. It has not, indeed, wholly escaped the foreign influences which Angevin rulers, with their crowds of "hated" Frenchmen, of a necessity imported. But the influence has been so slight, as to leave the plant practically uninjured; and while in its onward course feudalism trampled out every form of free government which had existed in Continental Europe[z], in England, thanks to the sturdy

[z] " Everywhere else [except in Switzerland] the ancient national assemblies have vanished altogether, or have been restored after a

resistance which the infusion of Scandinavian blood evoked, the curse of feudal institutions has been superseded by the self-government of a free people.

Feudalism in England, Norway, and Iceland.

§ 58. In England the Teutonic form of constitutional government has at last triumphed over every obstacle, and resulted in the well-balanced and perfectly-organised sway of King, Lords and Commons. This result is due to the stern rule of the Conqueror[a], who, while welding the nation together, and arousing its latent spirit and energies by a despotic rule, so firmly established the principle of monarchy, that it never afterwards succumbed, as it did on the Continent, to the disorganised rule of a number of petty despots[b]. His severity, following close upon the steps of the Danish conquerors, checked the career of a feudalism very similar to that which has already been traced in Iceland. Under Eadgar the nation had, as it seemed, been brought into harmony and unity; but it was more in appearance than in reality, as the events following his death too plainly shewed. His administration and personal supervision of his kingdom was able and indefatigable; his legislation was upright. But the direct effect was to increase the power of the great lords. The evil days which

while under forms wholly different from those of earlier days. In England, though the nature of our national assemblies has greatly changed, it has changed step by step; there has been no pulling down, no rebuilding."—Freeman, Norm. C., v. 387.

[a] Cp. Stubbs, C. H., i. 24.

[b] The whole of the Conqueror's policy aimed at defeating the disruptive tendencies of feudal institutions. Stubbs, C. H., i. 267.

his death brought upon the nation shewed the weak point in his system to have been "centralization without concentration[c]." Hence there was danger that the great lords, now no longer restrained by the curb of a strong ruler, would ruin the country by intestine wars, consequent on the extension of their own rights and the assertion of their independence. Had these events been permitted to develope themselves, as in Iceland, to their full extent, the result to the country must have been disastrous. But soon came the renewal of the Danish invasions, which inspired the nation, as it were, with a new life, and prepared it to accept the restoration of national unity from the measures of stern repression adopted by the Conqueror. Thus in the end the distracted anarchy of the latter half of the tenth century worked for the good of the nation. In the general disruption of society the seeds of individual liberty were preserved for happier days, when concentration, as well as centralisation, could bind together in harmonious working order the shattered fragments of the nation. "The national unity," to use Professor Stubbs' words, "was weakened by the sense of provincial unity, and individual liberty was strengthened against the time when the national unity should be, not the centralisation of powers, but the concentration of all organisation; a period long distant, and to be reached through strange vicissitudes[d]." In Norway, events shaped themselves somewhat analogously. On a country

[c] Stubbs, C. H., i. 209.   [d] Ibid.

split up into countless independent kingships, with little or no unity, a powerful king succeeded in imposing a strong monarchical rule. The feudal tenure which he sought to introduce by the imposition of a Landscatt on the allodial böndar has in the long run failed of success. Nor, owing partly to national customs, but chiefly to physical causes[e], did the main link in the feudal chain—a feudal nobility—succeed in establishing itself under the sovereignty of the monarch; and to the present day the constitution of Norway is rather a free democracy under a popular sovereign, than constitutional in our sense of the term. In Iceland, on the contrary, the freedom from all external control permitted the full development of those northern principles of self-dependence and individualism, which in Norway the introduction of monarchy had checked. And to what did they lead? To anarchy and confusion, resulting in the oppression of the people. Paradoxical as it seems, it is a fact that the worst sort of feudalism was the legitimate outcome of those same principles of freedom and self-government, which the men who colonised Iceland cherished too highly to relinquish for a more settled form of government. For what are the chief features of feudalism, but the absence of any sufficient guarantee for the maintenance of private rights and public institutions[f]? The in-

[e] Amongst these may be especially noticed, the absence of towns and fortified strongholds. Cf. Laing, " Sea-Kings of Norway," vol. i.

[f] " The tendency of feudalism is to a divided land, with a weak

stitutions may be, to all appearance, free; the rights of individuals may seem to be secured, but without a guarantee there is no real freedom. Such guarantee must be either a central dominant force—the strong will of a powerful monarch, or a strong public will—the resultant of individual wills, the concentration of the individual forces working in the nation, which will be equally respected by all, and can exert its just influence upon all alike. It was the absence of any such guarantee which formed the distinguishing mark of the Icelandic commonwealth. As in the French feudal polity, so in the Icelandic, there was an entire absence of all supreme legislation [g]. No foreign force intervening in Iceland, the disruptive tendencies of such an organisation had full play, and the conclusion was inevitable.

§ 59. To make this yet clearer, it is desirable to look more closely into the nature of the feudal relation; for it has been urged by some [h] that feudalism did not, and could not exist in Scandinavia, because the germs from which the feudal organisation was evolved on the Continent were absent from the Scandinavian polity. The full development of feudal tenures and feudal government did not exist in Iceland, and probably never could have existed there, because not all the necessary conditions were present. The effect of Roman

Analysis of Feudalism.

central government, or no central government at all."—Freeman, Norm. C., v. 367. Cp. Guizot, Civilisation en Europe.

[g] Hallam, M. A., i. 212. [h] e.g. Laing.

law played an important part in the feudalism of the Continent, and the combination of Roman influence with Teutonic institutions resulted in French feudalism [i]. Roman influence had no place in the Scandinavian polity, and therefore the result, such as we trace it on the Continent, is not to be looked for in Iceland. Again, the Icelanders were, so far as other nations were concerned, an eminently peaceful community. They used to take service under foreign leaders, and get their fair share in harrying other lands. But they were never as a nation engaged in constant warfare with others; and consequently, that aspect of feudalism which is distinctly military, and which sprang from the necessity of constant military preparation and organisation on the Continent, was wanting in Iceland. But pure feudal principles have a deeper root than the mere concurrence and amalgamation of two different systems; and the main ingredients of feudalism are based upon principles common to every distracted state of society, viz. the need of the weak for the protection of the strong, and the necessity of some security for public order [k].

What, then, does an analysis of feudalism tell us as to its nature and origin? The germs of feudalism were partly of Teutonic and partly of Roman origin; for feudalism, as Professor Stubbs [l] points out, grew up from two great sources,—the beneficium, and the practice of commendation. These

---

[i] Cp. Stubbs.   [k] Hallam, M. A., i. 164.
[l] C. H., i. 252.

two elements, of which the former is "partly of Roman, partly of German origin," and the latter apparently of Gallic or Celtic origin [m], in conjunction with the German comitatus (which, however, in origin "is to be carefully distinguished from the other two,") found in "the conquered soil of Roman Gaul" a combination of favourable influences, which fostered their development into the "jurisprudence of the Middle Ages."

The description of these two elements we must borrow from Professor Stubbs [n]: "The beneficiary system originated partly in gifts of land made by the kings out of their own estates to their kinsmen and servants, with a special undertaking to be faithful: partly in the surrender by landowners of their estates to churches or powerful men, to be received back again and held by them as tenants for rent or service. By the latter arrangement the weaker man obtained the protection of the stronger, and he who felt himself insecure placed his title under the defence of the Church. By the practice of commendation, on the other hand, the inferior put himself under the personal care of a lord, but without altering his title or divesting himself of his right to his estate; he became a vassal and did homage."

§ 60. Now the question to be decided is, whether there existed in Iceland any customs or institutions

Elements of Feudalism in Iceland.

---

[m] "Commendation may have had a Gallic or Celtic origin, and an analogy only with the Roman clientship."—Stubbs, C. H., l. c.

[n] C. H., i. 252, 253.

analogous to the above, and from which feudal principles might naturally be evolved; and whether the conditions of the state of society in Iceland in the tenth to the thirteenth centuries were such as to render such feudal relations necessary. For if it can be shewn that such elements did exist, our conclusion as to the natural evolution of a feudal state from the Icelandic polity will receive material confirmation. As to the latter point, enough has already been said to shew that public security was by no means inherent in the Icelandic community. A most glaring instance of the insecurity of a man in his own house is afforded by the murderous attack on Hauskuld, priest of Whiteness. And in reference to the former, there were prevalent in Iceland several customs of a distinctly feudal character, which can leave us in no doubt as to the general tendency of the island; and which bear a close similarity to customs existing among the feudal nations of the Continent. The first of these is to be found in the peculiar mutual relations of the Goði and his Thingmen, which, however, have been so fully entered into already, that a bare reference to the analogy between the *traust* of the Icelandic þingmaðr, and the *trustis* of the Frank Antrustion will suffice in this place. Secondly, there existed in Iceland a very curious practice, called *arfsal*, or cession of one's own property, or right of inheritance, to another man, on condition of getting succour and support for life. "In the time of the Commonwealth 'arfsal' had a political sense, and was a sort of clientela. The chiefs caused rich persons, freedmen, and monied men of low birth, to bequeath to them all their wealth, and in return supported them in lawsuits during life[o]." The similarity of this practice to those customs which constituted the chief elements in Continental feudalism, is too striking to be overlooked. But we do not deduce the one from the other. Iceland, of all countries, was absolutely free from the influence of ancient Rome. We contend that it had its origin (as Mr. Hallam points out in the case of Commendation[p],) in the two very general principles above mentioned, viz. the need of the weak for protection, and the necessity of maintaining public order, both of which the distracted state of society inculcated. Thirdly, the same may be said of another and not wholly dissimilar practice called *barnfóstr*, or adoption. It was a standing custom in the Sagas at bjóða e-m barnfóstr, to offer adoption to another man. "Men of wealth," says Mr. Vigfússon, "but of low birth, in order to get security for their property, offered barnfóstr to noblemen." It was not (as was the custom of arfsal) regarded as humiliating; but as it was considered a sort of homage to be foster-father of another man's son, it was not unfrequently done as a matter of policy, or even out of respect to another person. Thus Njál took Hauskuld to be his foster-son, in order to atone for the slaying of his father. And Ari Froði tells us in his "Islendingabók," that he was himself adopted

[o] Vigf., s. v.   [p] Supr., p. 134, note k.

by Hall of Hawkdale. Such fostering did not, however, imply the adoption of a son in the modern sense of the term. For adoption of a person as one's own son was permissible only in the case of an illegitimate child.

It is probable that in the palmy days of the Commonwealth, before the Sturlung period, the political results accruing from these semi-feudal relations were but small. But when the accumulation of Goðorðs began to lead to territorial sovereignty, and this in turn to some kind of feudal land-tenure (for after the union with Norway we find the Goðorðs were transferred to the king), it can hardly be doubted that the rival chiefs should have used every means in their power to bind their retainers to their service.

Development of Feudalism in Iceland different from Continental Feudalism.

§ 61. We have thus traced the action of one cause, or set of causes, which contributed to the development of feudalism in Iceland, and which was common as well to southern branches of the race. These and analogous causes at work among the Teutonic communities of the Continent, all tending in one direction, viz., inequality in the distribution of land, were, as Sir Henry Maine points out, of primitive growth [q]. But the full development of Continental feudalism is due to other causes as well; which were absent in the case of Iceland. These " shewed themselves when powerful Teutonic monarchies began to be formed, and consisted in grants of national waste land, or the soil of cou-

[q] Village Communities, chap. v.

quered provinces." These were the causes which combined most readily with the Roman influence yet existing in France, and out of which French feudalism grew up. That influence consisted, not merely in the active influence of Roman law and Roman practices working upon the Frank Constitution; but also in the fact, that the soil in which it was planted had been rendered congenial to the development of such a system by the action of the Imperial Government of Rome. "We see in it," writes Professor Stubbs[r], "the German system, modified by its work of foreign conquest, and deprived of its home safeguards, on a field exceptionally favourable, prepared and levelled by Roman agency under a civil system which was capable of speedy amalgamation, and into whose language most of the feudal forms readily translated themselves." Hence the difference between the form of feudalism developed in Iceland, and that "system which we are compelled to call feudalism," which on the Continent for years embraced every department of life, and which, though under it neither universal order nor universal liberty could subsist, yet in an age of anarchy and confusion laid the foundations of future order and freedom, by establishing the right of personal resistance, protected the tender shoots of a renascent literature, and gave birth to chivalry. Nor is it surprising, to use Sir H. Maine's words, "that there should have been a completer constitution of feudalism, in the countries which,

[r] Const. Hist., i. 4.

at the time of the conquest (by the Teutons), were filled with Romanised populations. The mould would be Teutonic, but the materials would be unusually plastic; and here would more specially come into play the influence of Roman law, giving precision to relations, which under purely Teutonic social conditions may have been in a high degree vague and indefinite."

Conclusion.

§ 62. It would be beyond the scope of the present essay to pursue this subject further, or trace the difference between the development of feudalism on English and on French soil. Enough has been said in the course of the preceding remarks, to shew the position which should be ascribed to Iceland in the History of European Institutions. An attempt has been made to trace the origin of feudalism to two sets of causes; the one of primitive growth, common to Scandinavia, as well as to the Teutons of the Continent; the second peculiar to the latter, and in part due to the influence of Rome. The development of feudalism from the former in Iceland has been described. It has been shewn how, in Iceland, isolated and cut off almost from the rest of the European family, these principles worked themselves out to their natural and logical consequences. An attempt has been made to shew how, while agreeing in the main with the primitive Teutonic organisation of the Continent, and containing in common with the latter like germs of future political institutions, the Scandinavian polity, transplanted from Norway beyond the reach of feudal influences, blossomed into perfection, and fell into decay. Hence Iceland, as affording to the historian a perfect specimen of one form of feudal evolution, entirely free, natural, and unimpeded by external influences, must rank high in the history of political institutions. The secret of modern scientific inquiry is to reduce to their simplest elements the complex forms which the history of civilised man presents; to analyse and compare the several systems of various nationalities, so as if possible to arrive at some general principles common to all. For such a scientific investigation the study of the institutions and literature of Iceland must furnish valuable data, by way of contrast, if not by way of analogy. Nor from a more particular point of view is Iceland less interesting to the English student. For though, as has been already shewn, no direct influence can be traced between the two countries, so far as political institutions are concerned; and though the direct influence of the Danes during the period of their occupation has been unduly exaggerated; yet, in respect of language, the importance of Iceland must not be underrated. Nor can it be doubted that England inherits from the race of men who colonised Iceland, both directly through the Northmen who visited and settled on British shores, and indirectly through the Norman Conquest, those sturdy qualities which have carried her sons triumphantly to every quarter of the globe; and enabled them to multiply throughout the world prosperous communities, possessing the same free and independent natures as their Scandinavian forefathers, and enjoying the blessings of those free institutions, and that "self-government," which seem peculiar to the Teutonic race.

APPENDIX A.

The Grágás.

A FEW words as to the true nature of the celebrated Grágás code may not be out of place, as considerable misconception as to its origin has prevailed. Thus Professor Paijkull, in his "Summer in Iceland[a]," says, "In 1118 a more complete code was introduced by Bergþór, who was lögsögumaðr at that time. This was subsequently the famous 'Grágás.'" But it has been established by Dr. Maurer, that Iceland had no code in the true sense of the term, till its union with Norway, when the *Ironside* was introduced. Still they had written laws in the latter days of the Republic, and these date from Bergþor's speakership, when "þat varð at framfara at þá vas scrifaðr vígsloðe ok margt annat í lögom[b]." This passage, says Dr. Maurer, refers not to *codification*, as has been generally supposed, but to the committal of oral laws to writing. The name Grágás, misapplied to this MS., has since been used as a collective name for all Icelandic laws framed before the union with Norway[c].

APPENDIX B.

On the þingfesti.

The origin of this practice is of course to be found in the patriarchal manner in which the country was settled. But the motive which ultimately led to its being formu-

[a] Barnard's Translation, p. 290.   [b] Islend., cap. 10.
[c] Cp. Vigf., s. v. Grágás.

lated as a law, and written down in the Gragás, may perhaps be traced to the desire, on grounds of public security, of having some mode of registration of the people. If this be so, it offers an interesting analogy to the practice which obtained in England, and which grew up into the law of Frankpledge. This, says Hallam[d], was devised by the wisdom of our English kings as a remedy against the disorderly condition of society. "No man could leave the shire to which he belonged without permission of its alderman. No man could be without a lord, on whom he depended; though he might quit his present patron, it was under the condition of engaging himself to another. If he failed in this, his kindred were bound to present him in the county court, and to name a lord for him themselves; otherwise, he might be seized by any one who met him as a robber." So in Iceland, it was lawful to *spyrja at þingfesti e-s*, i.e. to call on a man to declare his þingfesti[e].

APPENDIX C.

Leið.

It is interesting to note the probable derivation of this word, which still exists in our Court-*leet*, i.e. the Court of the Hundred. Dr. Maurer says[f] it is the A.-S. láð, Engl. *lode*, or way, (cp. old Engl. *lodesman* = pilot); and explains that the meeting was held on the way home from the Althing by the Goðar. "Der Name Leið, d. h. Weg, scheint sich am besten daraus zu erklären, dass die Versammlung *eben auf dem Heimweg vom Allding* von den Goden gehalten wurde." But it is difficult to see how

---

[d] Mid. Ages, ii. 291. Schlegel, i. 159.
[e] Cf. Grágás, þingskap, § 3;
[f] Beitr., p. 169.

this could have been, for "the leið is not to be held earlier than fourteen nights after the conclusion of the Althing [g]." "Eð þat skal vera fjortán nóttun eptir vápnatak." Mr. Vigfússon says that Leið in this sense is not the same as leið = road, but "is akin to, if not derived from, the A.-S. liða, the name of a double month, June and July ;" at the end of the latter of which the leið would be held. The leið, it may here be added, though unknown to the earlier Norse law, is yet mentioned in the later laws of Norway. Hence it was probably adopted first in Iceland, and was only later introduced into Norway. Its institution arose it may be out of the necessities of the country, the difficulties of communication, &c., combined with the absence of printing. Since writing the above, I find that Schlegel, Grágás xcii., rejects the first derivation on the same grounds as those stated above; and at the same time suggests another, viz. the verb *at leita* = to inquire, which certainly accords with the business of the Court.

APPENDIX D.

Skapti's Law relating to Murder.

There is a passage relating to murder in the Islendingabók (cap. 8) which deserves notice. It is there stated, that Skapti, the Speaker, who introduced Njál's Fifth Court Law, passed also another law, "at engi vegandi skylði lysa víg a'hendr öðrom manne en ser, en áðr vóro her slík lög of þat sem í Norege." The exact meaning of this passage is much disputed, and, at any rate, admits of more than one interpretation. Literally translated, it means, "That no slayer shall charge any other person

[g] Grág. as quoted by Maur., Beitr., p. 172.

with manslaughter than himself; for, before this, the law with us was the same as in Norway." The Norse law, here referred to, being apparently that from the Gulathing Code (*supra*, p. 78). For the several interpretations which have been given, we may refer to Th. Möbius' note to the passage [h]. The object of the enactment seems clearly to be, to prevent a criminal from falsely charging another with the crime of which he is himself guilty; which might easily be done in the case of an affray, where the slayer had inflicted more than one wound on his victim [i]; cp. Njála, ch. cxi., where, in the proceedings consequent on Hauskuld's death, "Mord shews the neighbours Hauskuld's wounds, and takes witness to the hurts, and names a man as the dealer of every wound save one, and *that he made as though he knew not who had dealt it, but that wound he had dealt himself.*"

APPENDIX E.

On Judges and Jury.

The judges in an Icelandic law-suit were, in some ways, much more like the English jury than the búakviðr. But, without at all assuming an immediate connexion between the two, the functions of the kviðr may not improperly be compared to those of a Grand Jury, or Jury of presentment, whose duty it is to decide whether there is a *true bill* to go before the common jury for trial. "We are summoned," so runs the verdict of the búakviðr in Flosi's trial, "to bear witness whether Flosi killed Njál's son." Not till after this verdict has been returned does the de-

---

[h] Isländerbuch, p. 32, n. 20.   [i] Das., ii. p. 114.

fendant begin his defence; and the subsequent judgment of the judges (dómendr) is given according as he succeeds or not. Again, the maxim, "De quæstionibus juris respondent Judices, de quæstionibus facti juratores," is distinctly laid down in Grág., c. 85 (Thingsk.): "Eigi eigu búar enn at bera um þat hvat lög eru á landiher," i.e., "the inquest have not to give verdict in (decide) what is law in the country." On the other hand, a jury had to fix the compensation due for damages, cf. Grágás, i. 383, &c. (Schleg.), "Bæta skal hann au-visli á fjórtán nóttun sem búar fimm virða." With respect to the change of character in English jurors (from witnesses to judges), may it not be traced to the change of moral feeling described in § 37? At first, the only question was a question of fact. Did he commit the act? Now, when motive and intention are taken into account, the evidence becomes very complicated, and often is wholly circumstantial. Hence the functions of the jury are no longer to give personal evidence, but to judge of difficult and often very conflicting evidence.

APPENDIX F.

The Exposure of Infants.

The exposure of infants was in Iceland a lawful act, but very seldom practised. It must take place immediately after birth, before the child has tasted *any* kind of food, and before it was sprinkled with water (ausa vatni), or shewn to the father, who had to fix its name. Exposure after any of these acts was murder. (Vigf., s. v. *bera út*.) It need not excite surprise that a practice common to all, or nearly all, heathen nations, should be found in Scandinavia. On the other hand, Tacitus tells us that, in the southern branch of the Teutonic family, it was regarded as a crime; if, indeed, this is the true meaning of the passage. "*Numerum liberorum finire aut quemquam ex agnatis (afterborn) necare flagitium habetur* [k]." From the Gunnlang Saga, cap. 3, we learn that it was regularly done by poor persons, who were already burdened with a large family, though "þótti þó illa gert ávallt," i.e., it was regarded with disapprobation.

As to the practice of eating horse-flesh, Laing is, doubtless, right in admitting it as evidence of the Asiatic origin of the Scandinavian Communities[1].

Germ. xix. [1] "Early Kings of Norway," i. p. 38.

CORRIGENDA.

Page 65, line 6, *for* Thing, *read* Thing."
 ,, 70, ,, 19, *for* decline, *read* declines.
 ,, 74, ,, 25, *for* Zunächst, *read* zunächts.
 ,, 75, ,, 12, *for* tólflar, *read* tólftar.
 ,, 76, ,, 1, *for* veltvangsbúar *read* vettvangsbúar.
 ,, 78, ,, 18, *for* em, *read* eru.
 ,, 79, ,, 30, *for* I. F. Stephen, *read* J. F. Stephen.
 ,, 86, ,, 8, *for* vetvangsbúas, *read* vettvangsbúar.
 ,, ,,   ,, 26, *for* ἐκκλησιά, *read* ἐκκλησία.
 ,, 95, ,, 24, *for* lýret at Goði, *read* lýrit af Goða.
 ,, ,,   ,, 25, *for* lýriti, *read* lýriti.
 ,, ,,   ,,   *for* þingskaþ, *read* þingskap.
 ,, 102, ,, 9, *dele* inverted commas.

Printed by James Parker and Co., Crown Yard, Oxford.

A SELECTION FROM THE PUBLICATIONS OF MESSRS. JAS. PARKER AND CO.

NEW BOOKS.

Keble's Commentaries.
COMMENTARIES ON THE INTRODUCTORY VERSES of St. John's Gospel, and on a portion of St. Paul's Epistle to the Romans; also an Analysis of St. Paul's Epistles, &c., &c., by the late Rev. JOHN KEBLE, M.A. 8vo., cloth, 10s. 6d.

Occasional Papers and Reviews,
On Sir Walter Scott, Poetry, and Sacred Poetry, Bishop Warburton, Rev. John Miller, Exeter Synod, Judicial Committee of Privy Council, Parochial Work, the Lord's Supper, Solomon, the Jewish Nation. By the late Rev. JOHN KEBLE, Author of "The Christian Year." 532 pp., with two Facsimiles from Common-place Book, Demy 8vo., cloth extra, 12s.

"They are prefaced by two letters of deep interest from Dr. NEWMAN and Dr. PUSEY. There is something extremely touching in the reunion, as it were, of the three old friends and fellow-labourers."—*Guardian*.

The First Prayer-book of Edward VI.
Compared with the Successive Revisions of the Book of Common Prayer. Together with a Concordance and Index to the Rubrics in the several Editions. Crown 8vo., cloth, 12s.

AN INTRODUCTION TO THE HISTORY OF THE Successive Revisions of the Book of Common Prayer. Crown 8vo., pp. xxxii., 532, cloth, 12s.

Offices of the Old Catholic Prayer-book.
A CATHOLIC RITUAL, published according to the Decrees of the First Two Synods of the Old Catholics of the German Empire. Done into English and compared with the Offices of the Roman and Old German Rituals. By the Rev. F. E. WARREN, B.D., Fellow of St. John's College, Oxford. Crown 8vo., cl., 3s. 6d.

The History of Confirmation.
By WILLIAM JACKSON, M.A., Queen's College, Oxford; Vicar of Heathfield, Sussex. Crown 8vo., cloth, 4s.

The Awaking Soul,
As sketched in the 130th Psalm. Addresses delivered at St. Peter's, Eaton-square, on the Tuesdays in Lent, 1877, by E. R. WILBERFORCE, M.A., Vicar of Seaforth, Liverpool; and Sub-Almoner to the Queen. Crown 8vo., limp cloth, 2s. 6d.

Stories from the Old Testament.
With Four Illustrations. Square crown 8vo., 4s.

Adams's Historical Tales.
TALES ILLUSTRATING CHURCH HISTORY. ENGLAND: Mediæval Period. By the Rev. H. C. ADAMS, Vicar of Dry Sandford; Author of "Wilton of Cuthbert's," "Schoolboy Honour," &c. With four Illustrations on Wood. Fcap. 8vo., cloth, 5s.

JAMES PARKER AND CO., OXFORD AND LONDON.

The Founder of Norwich Cathedral.

The LIFE, LETTERS, and SERMONS of BISHOP HERBERT DE LOSINGA (*b. circ.* A.D. 1050, *d.* 1119), the LETTERS (as translated by the Editors) being incorporated into the LIFE, and the SERMONS being now first edited from a MS. in the possession of the University of Cambridge, and accompanied with an English Translation and English Notes. By EDWARD MEYRICK GOULBURN, D.D., Dean of Norwich, and HENRY SYMONDS, M.A., Rector of Tivetshall, and late Precentor of Norwich Cathedral. 2 vols. 8vo., cloth, 24s. [*Shortly.*

Vincent of Lerins Against Heresy.

VINCENTIUS LIRINENSIS ADVERSUS OMNES HÆRETICORUM NOVITATES COMMONITORIUM. Editio Tertio. In Latin and English. Fcap. 8vo.

The Place of Iceland in the History of European Institutions:

Being the Lothian Prize Essay, 1877. By C. A. VANSITTART CONYBEARE, B.A., late Junior Student of Christ Church, Oxford; and Assistant Master at Manchester Grammar-School. Crown 8vo.

The Archæology of Rome,

THE ARCHÆOLOGY OF ROME. By JOHN HENRY PARKER, C.B.

THE TOMBS IN AND NEAR ROME, with the Columbaria and the Painted Tombs on the Via Latina, with Twenty-four Plates in Photo-engraving.

MYTHOLOGY IN FUNEREAL SCULPTURE, and Early Christian Sculpture, with Sixteen Plates. *These two Parts in one Volume.* Medium 8vo., cloth, 15s.

THE CATACOMBS, OR ANCIENT CEMETERIES OF ROME, with Twenty-four Plates and Plans. Medium 8vo., cloth, 15s.

The Catholic Doctrine of the Sacrifice and Participation of the Holy Eucharist.

By GEORGE TREVOR, M.A., D.D., Canon of York; Rector of Beeford. Second Edition, Revised and Enlarged. Crown 8vo., cloth, 10s. 6d.

The Annals of England:

AN EPITOME OF ENGLISH HISTORY, from Contemporary Writers, the Rolls of Parliament, and other Public Records. A LIBRARY EDITION, revised and enlarged, with additional Woodcuts. 8vo., cloth, 12s.

THE SCHOOL EDITION of THE ANNALS of ENGLAND. In Five Half-crown Parts. 1. Britons, Romans, Saxons, Normans. 2. The Plantagenets. 3. The Tudors. 4. The Stuarts. 5. The Restoration, to the Death of Queen Anne. Fcap. 8vo., cloth.

The Exile from Paradise.

Translated by the Author of the "Life of S. Teresa." Fcap., cloth, 1s. 6d.

JAMES PARKER AND CO.

Daniel the Prophet.

Nine Lectures delivered in the Divinity School, Oxford. With a Short Preface in Answer to Dr. Rowland Williams. By E. B. PUSEY, D.D., Regius Professor of Hebrew, and Canon of Christ Church. *Seventh Thousand.* 8vo., 10s. 6d.

The Minor Prophets;

With a Commentary Explanatory and Practical, and Introductions to the Several Books. By the Rev. E. B. PUSEY, D.D., &c. 4to., cloth, price £1 11s. 6d.

The Fifty-third Chapter of Isaiah,

According to the Jewish Interpreters. I. Texts edited from Printed Books, and MSS., by AD. NEUBAUER. Price 18s. II. Translations by S. R. DRIVER and AD. NEUBAUER. With an Introduction to the Translations by the Rev. E. B. PUSEY, Regius Professor of Hebrew, Oxford. Post 8vo., cloth, 12s.

The Prophecies of Isaiah.

Their Authenticity and Messianic Interpretation Vindicated, in a Course of Sermons preached before the University of Oxford. By the Very Rev. R. PAYNE SMITH, D.D., Dean of Canterbury. 8vo., cloth, 10s. 6d.

A Plain Commentary on the Book of Psalms

(Prayer-book Version), chiefly grounded on the Fathers. For the Use of Families. 2 vols., Fcap. 8vo., cloth, 10s. 6d.

The Psalter and the Gospel.

The Life, Sufferings, and Triumph of our Blessed Lord, revealed in the Book of Psalms. Fcap. 8vo., cloth, 2s.

A Summary of the Evidences for the Bible.

By the Rev. T. S. ACKLAND, M.A., late Fellow of Clare Hall, Cambridge; Incumbent of Pollington cum Balne, Yorkshire. 24mo., cloth, 3s.

Godet's Biblical Studies

ON THE OLD TESTAMENT. Edited by the Hon. and Rev. W. H. LYTTELTON, Rector of Hagley, and Honorary Canon of Worcester. Fcap. 8vo. cloth, price 6s.

Catena Aurea.

A Commentary on the Four Gospels, collected out of the Works of the Fathers by S. THOMAS AQUINAS. Uniform with the Library of the Fathers. A Re-issue, complete in 6 vols., cloth, £2 2s.

A Plain Commentary on the Four Holy Gospels,

Intended chiefly for Devotional Reading. By the Very Rev. J. W. BURGON, B.D., Dean of Chichester. New Edition. 4 vols., Fcap. 8vo., limp cloth, £1 1s.

The Last Twelve Verses of the Gospel according to S. Mark

Vindicated against Recent Critical Objectors and Established, by the Very Rev. J. W. BURGON, B.D., Dean of Chichester. With Facsimiles of Codex ℵ and Codex L. 8vo., cloth, 12s.

The Gospels from a Rabbinical Point of View,

Shewing the perfect Harmony of the Four Evangelists on the subject of our Lord's Last Supper, and the Bearing of the Laws and Customs of the Jews at the time of our Lord's coming on the Language of the Gospels. By the Rev. G. WILDON PIERITZ, M.A. Crown 8vo., limp cloth, 3s.

Christianity as Taught by S. Paul.

By WILLIAM J. IRONS, D.D., of Queen's College, Oxford; Prebendary of S. Paul's; being the BAMPTON LECTURES for the Year 1870, with an Appendix of the CONTINUOUS SENSE of S. Paul's Epistles; with Notes and Metalegomena, 8vo., with Map, Second Edition, with New Preface, cloth, 9s.

S. Paul's Epistles to the Ephesians and Philippians.

A Practical and Exegetical Commentary. Edited by the late Rev. HENRY NEWLAND. 8vo., cloth, 7s. 6d.

A History of the Church,

From the Edict of Milan, A.D. 313, to the Council of Chalcedon, A.D. 451. By WILLIAM BRIGHT, D.D., Regius Professor of Ecclesiastical History, and Canon of Christ Church, Oxford. Second Edition. Post 8vo., 10s. 6d.

The Age of the Martyrs;

Or, The First Three Centuries of the Work of the Church of our Lord and Saviour Jesus Christ. By the late JOHN DAVID JENKINS, B.D., Fellow of Jesus College, Oxford; Canon of Pieter Maritzburg. Cr. 8vo., cl., reduced to 3s. 6d.

The Councils of the Church,

From the Council of Jerusalem, A.D. 51, to the Council of Constantinople, A.D. 381; chiefly as to their Constitution, but also as to their Objects and History. By E. B. PUSEY, D.D. 8vo., cloth, 6s.

The Ecclesiastical History of the First Three Centuries,

From the Crucifixion of Jesus Christ to the year 313. By the late Rev. Dr. BURTON. Fourth Edition. 8vo., cloth, 12s.

A Brief History of the Christian Church,

From the First Century to the Reformation. By the Rev. J. S. BARTLETT. Fcap. 8vo., cloth, 2s. 6d.

Manual of Ecclesiastical History,

From the First to the Twelfth Century inclusive. By the Rev. E. S. FFOULKES, M.A. 8vo., cloth, 6s.

A History of the English Church,

From its Foundation to the Reign of Queen Mary. By MARY CHARLOTTE STAPLEY. Third Edition, revised, with a Recommendatory Notice by DEAN HOOK. Crown 8vo., cloth, 5s.

Bede's Ecclesiastical History of the English Nation.

A New Translation by the Rev. L. GIDLEY, M.A., Chaplain of St. Nicholas', Salisbury. Crown 8vo., cloth, 6s.

OXFORD, AND 377, STRAND, LONDON.

The Principles of Divine Service;

Or, An Inquiry concerning the True Manner of Understanding and Using the Order for Morning and Evening Prayer, and for the Administration of the Holy Communion in the English Church. By the late Ven. PHILIP FREEMAN, M.A., Archdeacon of Exeter, &c. 2 vols. 8vo., cloth, 16s.

A History of the Book of Common Prayer,

And other Authorized Books, from the Reformation; with an Account of the State of Religion in England from 1640 to 1660. By the Rev. THOMAS LATHBURY, M.A. Second Edition, with an Index. 8vo., cloth, 10s. 6d.

Catechetical Lessons on the Book of Common Prayer.

Illustrating the Prayer-book, from its Title-page to the end of the Collects, Epistles, and Gospels. Designed to aid the Clergy in Public Catechising. By the Rev. Dr. FRANCIS HESSEY, Incumbent of St. Barnabas, Kensington, Fcap. 8vo., cloth, 6s.

A Short Explanation of the Nicene Creed,

For the Use of Persons beginning the Study of Theology. By the late A. P. FORBES, D.C.L., Bishop of Brechin. Second Edition, Crown 8vo., cloth, 6s.

An Explanation of the Thirty-Nine Articles.

By the late A. P. FORBES, D.C.L., Bishop of Brechin. With an Epistle Dedicatory to the Rev. E. B. PUSEY, D.D. Second Edition, in one vol., Post 8vo., 12s.

Addresses to the Candidates for Ordination on the Questions in the Ordination Service.

By the late SAMUEL WILBERFORCE, LORD BISHOP OF WINCHESTER. Fifth Thousand. Crown 8vo., cloth, 6s.

A Commentary on the Epistles and Gospels in the Book of Common Prayer.

Extracted from Writings of the Fathers of the Holy Catholic Church, anterior to the Division of the East and West. With an Introductory Notice by the DEAN OF ST. PAUL'S. 2 vols., Crown 8vo., cloth, 15s.

Sunday-School Exercises,

Collected and Revised from Manuscripts of Burghclere School-children, under the teaching of the Rev. W. B. BARTER, late Rector of Highclere and Burghclere; Edited by his Son-in-law, the BISHOP OF ST. ANDREW'S. Second Edition, Crown 8vo., cloth, 5s.

On Eucharistical Adoration.

With Considerations suggested by a Pastoral Letter on the Doctrine of the Most Holy Eucharist. By the late Rev. JOHN KEBLE, M.A., Vicar of Hursley. 24mo., sewed, 2s.

The Administration of the Holy Spirit

IN THE BODY OF CHRIST. The Bampton Lectures for 1868. By the Right Rev. the LORD BISHOP OF SALISBURY. *Second Edition.* Crown 8vo., 7s. 6d.

Sayings ascribed to our Lord

By the Fathers and other Primitive Writers, and Incidents in His Life narrated by them, otherwise than found in Scripture. By JOHN THEODORE DODD, B.A., late Junior Student of Christ Church. Crown 8vo., cloth, 3s.

The Pastoral Rule of S. Gregory.
Sancti Gregorii Papæ Regulæ Pastoralis Liber, ad JOHANNEM, Episcopum Civitatis Ravennæ. With an English Translation. By the Rev. H. R. BRAMLEY, M.A., Fellow of Magdalen College, Oxford. Fcap. 8vo., cloth, 6s.

The Canons of the Church.
The Definitions of the Catholic Faith and Canons of Discipline of the First Four General Councils of the Universal Church. In Greek and English. Fcap. 8vo., cloth, 2s. 6d.

The English Canons.
The Constitutions and Canons Ecclesiastical of the Church of England, referred to their Original Sources, and Illustrated with Explanatory Notes, by MACKENZIE E. C. WALCOTT, B.D., F.S.A., Præcentor and Prebendary of Chichester. Fcap. 8vo., cloth, 4s.

Vincentius Lirinensis
For the Antiquity and Universality of the Catholic Faith against the Profane Novelties of all Heretics. Latin and English. New Edition, Fcap. 8vo. [*Nearly ready.*]
Translation only. 18mo., 1s. 6d.

De Fide et Symbolo:
Documenta quædam nec non Aliquorum SS. Patrum Tractatus. Edidit CAROLUS A. HEURTLEY, S.T.P., Dom. Margaretæ Prælector, et Ædis Christi Canonicus. Fcap. 8vo., cloth, 4s. 6d.

The Athanasian Creed.
A Critical History of the Athanasian Creed, by the Rev. DANIEL WATERLAND, D.D. Fcap. 8vo., cloth, 5s.

St. Cyril, Archbishop of Alexandria.
The Three Epistles (ad Nestorium, ii., iii., et ad Joan Antioch). A Revised Text, with an old Latin Version and an English Translation. Edited by P. E. PUSEY, M.A. 8vo., in wrapper, 3s.

S. Aurelius Augustinus,
EPISCOPUS HIPPONENSIS,
De Catechizandis Rudibus, de Fide Rerum quæ non videntur, de Utilitate Credendi. In Usum Juniorum. Edidit C. MARRIOTT, S.T.B., olim Coll. Oriel. Socius. A New Edition, Fcap. 8vo., cloth, 3s. 6d.

Cur Deus Homo,
Or Why God was made Man; by ST. ANSELM. Translated into English, with an Introduction, &c. Fcap. 8vo., 2s. 6d.
Latin and English Edition *nearly ready.*

The Book of Ratramn
The Priest and Monk of Corbey, commonly called Bertram, on the Body and Blood of the Lord. (Latin and English.) To which is added AN APPENDIX, containing the Saxon Homily of Ælfric. Fcap. 8vo. [*Nearly ready.*]

NEW AND CHEAPER ISSUE

OF

The Library of the Fathers

OF THE HOLY CATHOLIC CHURCH, ANTERIOR TO THE DIVISION OF THE EAST AND WEST.

Translated by Members of the English Church.

Already Issued.

St. Athanasius against the Arians. 1 vol., 10s. 6d.
────────────── Historical Tracts } 10s. 6d.
────────────── Festal Epistles   }
St. Augustine's Confessions, with Notes, 6s.
────────────── Sermons on the New Testament. 2 vols., 15s.
────────────── Homilies on the Psalms. 6 vols., £2 2s.
────────────── on the Gospel and First Epistle of St. John. 2 vols., 15s.
────────────── Practical Treatises. 6s.
St. Chrysostom's Homilies on the Gospel of St. Matthew. 3 vols., £1 1s.
────────────── Homilies on the Gospel of St. John. 2 vols., 14s.
────────────── Homilies on the Acts of the Apostles. 2 vols., 12s.
────────────── to the People of Antioch. 7s. 6d.
────────────── Homilies on St. Paul's Epistle to the Romans. 1 vol., 6s.   [*Just ready.*
St. Cyprian's Treatises and Epistles, with the Treatises of St. Pacian. 10s.
St. Cyril (Bishop of Jerusalem), Catechetical Lectures on the Creed and Sacraments. 7s.
St. Cyril (Archbishop of Alexandria), Commentary upon the Gospel of St. John. Vol. I. 8s.
St. Ephrem's Rhythms on the Nativity, and on Faith. 8s. 6d.
St. Gregory the Great, Morals on the Book of Job. 4 vols., £1 11s. 6d.
St. Irenæus, the Works of. 8s.
St. Justin the Martyr. Works now extant. 6s.
Tertullian's Apologetical and Practical Treatises. 9s.

The following may still be had in the original bindings :—

St. Chrysostom's Homilies on St. Paul's Epistles to the Corinthians. 2 vols., 18s.
────────────── Timothy, Titus, and Philemon. 1 vol., 7s. 6d.

JAMES PARKER AND CO.

Works of the Standard English Divines,

PUBLISHED IN THE LIBRARY OF ANGLO-CATHOLIC THEOLOGY,

At the following prices in Cloth.

Andrewes' (Bp.) Complete Works. 11 vols., 8vo., £3 7s.
    The Sermons. (Separate.) 5 vols., £1 15s.

Beveridge's (Bp.) Complete Works. 12 vols., 8vo., £4 4s.
    The English Theological Works. 10 vols., £3 10s.

Bramhall's (Abp.) Works, with Life and Letters, &c. 5 vols., 8vo., £1 15s.

Bull's (Bp.) Harmony on Justification. 2 vols., 8vo., 10s.
——————— **Defence of the Nicene Creed.** 2 vols., 10s.
——————— **Judgment of the Catholic Church.** 5s.

Cosin's (Bp.) Works Complete. 5 vols., 8vo., £1 10s.

Crakanthorp's Defensio Ecclesiæ Anglicanæ. 8vo., 7s.

Frank's Sermons. 2 vols., 8vo., 10s.

Forbes' Considerationes Modestæ. 2 vols., 8vo., 12s.

Gunning's Paschal, or Lent Fast. 8vo., 6s.

Hammond's Practical Catechism. 8vo., 5s.
——————— **Miscellaneous Theological Works.** 5s.
——————— **Thirty-one Sermons.** 2 Parts. 10s.

Hickes's Two Treatises on the Christian Priesthood. 3 vols., 8vo., 15s.

Johnson's (John) Theological Works. 2 vols., 8vo., 10s.
——————— **English Canons.** 2 vols., 12s.

Laud's (Abp.) Complete Works. 7 vols., (9 Parts,) 8vo., £2 17s.

L'Estrange's Alliance of Divine Offices. 8vo., 6s.

Marshall's Penitential Discipline. 8vo., 4s.

Nicholson's (Bp.) Exposition of the Catechism. (This volume cannot be sold separate from the complete set.)

Overall's (Bp.) Convocation-book of 1606. 8vo., 5s.

Pearson's (Bp.) Vindiciæ Epistolarum S. Ignatii. 2 vols., 8vo., 10s.

Thorndike's (Herbert) Theological Works Complete. 6 vols., (10 Parts,) 8vo., £2 10s.

Wilson's (Bp.) Works Complete. With Life, by Rev. J. Keble. 7 vols., (8 Parts,) 8vo., £3 3s.

The Catechist's Manual;
With an Introduction by the late SAMUEL WILBERFORCE, LORD BISHOP OF WINCHESTER. 5th Thousand. Cr. 8vo., limp cl., 5s.

The Confirmation Class-book:
Notes for Lessons, with APPENDIX, containing Questions and Summaries for the Use of the Candidates. By EDWARD M. HOLMES, LL.B., Author of the "Catechist's Manual." Fcap. 8vo., limp cloth, 2s. 6d.

    THE QUESTIONS, separate, 4 sets, in wrapper, 1s.
    THE SUMMARIES, separate, 4 sets, in wrapper, 1s.

The Church's Work in our Large Towns.
By GEORGE HUNTINGTON, M.A., Rector of Tenby, and Domestic Chaplain of the Rt. Hon. the Earl of Crawford and Balcarres. Second Edit., revised and enlarged. Cr. 8vo., cl. 3s. 6d.

The Church and the School:
Containing Practical Hints on the Work of a Clergyman. By H. W. BELLAIRS, M.A., One of Her Majesty's Inspectors of Schools. Cheap re-issue, Crown 8vo., limp cloth, 2s. 6d.

Notes of Seven Years' Work in a Country Parish.
By R. F. WILSON, M.A., Prebendary of Sarum, and Examining Chaplain to the Bishop of Salisbury. Fcap. 8vo., cloth, 4s.

A Manual of Pastoral Visitation,
Intended for the Use of the Clergy in their Visitation of the Sick and Afflicted. By A PARISH PRIEST. Dedicated, by permission, to His Grace the Archbishop of Dublin. Second Edition, Crown 8vo., limp cloth, 3s. 6d.; roan, 4s.

The Cure of Souls.
By the Rev. G. ARDEN, M.A., Rector of Winterborne-Came, and Author of "Breviates from Holy Scripture," &c. Fcap. 8vo., cloth, 2s. 6d.

Questions on the Collects, Epistles, and Gospels,
Throughout the Year. Edited by the Rev. T. L. CLAUGHTON, Vicar of Kidderminster. For the Use of Teachers in Sunday Schools. Fifth Edition, 18mo., cl. In two Parts, *each* 2s. 6d.

Pleas for the Faith.
Especially designed for the use of Missionaries at Home and Abroad. By the Rev. W. SOMERVILLE LACH SZYRMA, M.A., St. Augustine's College, Canterbury. Fcap. 8vo., cl., 2s. 6d.

JAMES PARKER AND CO.

MEDITATIONS FOR THE FORTY DAYS OF LENT.
With a Prefatory Notice by the ARCHBISHOP OF DUBLIN. 18mo., cloth, 2s. 6d.

DAILY STEPS TOWARDS HEAVEN;
Or, PRACTICAL THOUGHTS on the GOSPEL HISTORY, and especially on the Life and Teaching of our Lord Jesus Christ, for Every Day in the Year, according to the Christian Seasons, with the Titles and Character of Christ, and a Harmony of the Four Gospels. Newly printed, with antique type. Fortieth thousand. 32mo., roan, gilt edges, 2s. 6d.; morocco, 5s.

LARGE-TYPE EDITION. Square Crown 8vo., cloth antique, red edges, 5s.

ANNUS DOMINI.
A Prayer for each Day of the Year, founded on a Text of Holy Scripture. By CHRISTINA G. ROSSETTI. 32mo., cl., 3s. 6d.

LITURGIA DOMESTICA:
Services for every Morning and Evening in the Week. Third Edition. 18mo., 2s. Or in two Parts, 1s. each.

EARL NELSON'S FAMILY PRAYERS.
With Responsions and Variations for the different Seasons, for General Use. New and improved Edition, *large type*, cloth, 2s.

OF THE IMITATION OF CHRIST.
Four Books. By THOMAS A KEMPIS. Small 4to., printed on thick toned paper, with red border-lines, mediæval title-pages, ornamental initials, &c. Third Thousand. Cloth, 12s.

PRAYERS FOR MARRIED PERSONS.
From Various Sources, chiefly from the Ancient Liturgies. Selected and Edited by CHARLES WARD, M.A., Rector of Maulden. Second Edition, Revised. 24mo., cloth, 4s. 6d.

FOR THE LORD'S SUPPER.
DEVOTIONS BEFORE AND AFTER HOLY COMMUNION. With Preface by J. KEBLE. Sixth Edition. 32mo., cloth, 2s. With the Office, cloth, 2s. 6d.

DEVOUT COMMUNION, from HORST. 18mo., cloth, 1s.

OFFICIUM EUCHARISTICUM. By EDWARD LAKE, D.D. New Edition. 32mo., cloth, 1s. 6d.

A SHORT AND PLAIN INSTRUCTION FOR THE BETTER UNDERSTANDING OF THE LORD'S SUPPER. By BISHOP WILSON. 32mo., with Rubrics, cloth, gilt edges, 2s.
————————— 32mo., limp cloth, 8d.; sewed, 6d.
————————— 24mo., limp cloth, 1s.

OXFORD, AND 377, STRAND, LONDON.

Oxford Editions of Devotional Works.

Fcap. 8vo., chiefly printed in Red and Black, on Toned Paper.

Andrewes' Devotions.
DEVOTIONS. By the Right Rev. LANCELOT ANDREWES. Translated from the Greek and Latin, and arranged anew. Cloth, 5s.

The Imitation of Christ.
FOUR BOOKS. By THOMAS A KEMPIS. A new Edition, revised. Cloth, 4s.

Laud's Devotions.
THE PRIVATE DEVOTIONS of Dr. WILLIAM LAUD, Archbishop of Canterbury, and Martyr. Antique cloth, 5s.

Spinckes' Devotions.
TRUE CHURCH OF ENGLAND MAN'S COMPANION IN THE CLOSET. By NATHANIEL SPINCKES. Floriated borders, antique cloth, 4s.

Sutton's Meditations.
GODLY MEDITATIONS UPON THE MOST HOLY SACRAMENT OF THE LORD'S SUPPER. By CHRISTOPHER SUTTON, D.D., late Prebend of Westminster. A new Edition. Antique cloth, 5s.

Taylor's Golden Grove.
THE GOLDEN GROVE: A Choice Manual, containing what is to be Believed, Practised, and Desired or Prayed for. By Bishop JEREMY TAYLOR. Antique cloth, 3s. 6d.

Taylor's Holy Living.
THE RULE AND EXERCISES OF HOLY LIVING. By Bishop JEREMY TAYLOR. Ant. cloth, 4s.

Taylor's Holy Dying.
THE RULE AND EXERCISES OF HOLY DYING. By Bishop JEREMY TAYLOR. Ant. cloth, 4s.

Wilson's Sacra Privata.
THE PRIVATE MEDITATIONS, DEVOTIONS, and PRAYERS of the Right Rev. T. WILSON, D.D., Lord Bishop of Sodor and Man. Now first printed entire. Cloth, 4s.

Ancient Collects.
ANCIENT COLLECTS AND OTHER PRAYERS, Selected for Devotional Use from various Rituals, with an Appendix on the Collects in the Prayerbook. By WILLIAM BRIGHT, D.D. Fourth Edition. Antique cloth, 5s.

Devout Communicant.
THE DEVOUT COMMUNICANT, exemplified in his Behaviour before, at, and after the Sacrament of the Lord's Supper: Practically suited to all the Parts of that Solemn Ordinance. 7th Edition, revised. Edited by Rev. G. MOULTRIE. Fcap. 8vo., toned paper, red lines, ant. cl., 4s.

ΕΙΚΩΝ ΒΑΣΙΛΙΚΗ.
THE PORTRAITURE OF HIS SACRED MAJESTY KING CHARLES I. in his Solitudes and Sufferings. Cloth, 5s.

JAMES PARKER AND CO.

THE AUTHORIZED EDITIONS OF
THE CHRISTIAN YEAR,
With the Author's latest Corrections and Additions.

NOTICE.—Messrs. PARKER are the sole Publishers of the Editions of the "Christian Year" issued with the sanction and under the direction of the Author's representatives. All Editions without their imprint are unauthorized.

	s. d.		s. d.
SMALL 4to. EDITION.		32mo. EDITION.	
Handsomely printed on toned paper, with red border lines and initial letters. Cl. extra	10 6	Cloth, limp	1 0
		Cloth boards, gilt edges	1 6
DEMY 8VO. EDITION.		48mo. EDITION.	
Cloth	6 0	Cloth, limp	0 6
		Cloth boards	0 9
FOOLSCAP 8VO. EDITION.		Roan	1 6
Cloth	3 6	FACSIMILE OF THE 1ST EDITION, with a list of the variations from the Original Text which the Author made in later Editions. 2 vols., 12mo., boards	7 6
24mo. EDITION.			
Cloth	2 0		
Ditto, with red lines	2 6		

The above Editions (except the Facsimile of the First Edition) are kept in a variety of bindings, the chief of which are Morocco plain, Morocco Antique, Calf Antique, and Vellum.

By the same Author.

LYRA INNOCENTIUM. Thoughts in Verse on Christian Children. *Thirteenth Edition.* Fcap. 8vo., cl., 5s.

———————— 48mo. edition, limp cloth, 6d.; cloth boards, 1s.

MISCELLANEOUS POEMS BY THE REV. JOHN KEBLE, M.A., Vicar of Hursley. *Third Edition.* Fcap., cloth, 6s.

THE PSALTER, OR PSALMS OF DAVID: In English Verse. *Fourth Edition.* Fcap., cloth, 6s.

The above may also be had in various bindings.

By the late Rev. ISAAC WILLIAMS.

THE CATHEDRAL; or, The Catholic and Apostolic Church in England. 32mo., cloth, 2s. 6d.

THE BAPTISTERY; or, The Way of Eternal Life, with Plates by BOETIUS A BOLSWERT. Fcap. 8vo., cloth, 7s. 6d.; 32mo., cloth, 2s. 6d.

HYMNS translated from the PARISIAN BREVIARY. 32mo., cloth, 2s. 6d.

THE CHRISTIAN SCHOLAR. Fcap. 8vo., cl., 5s.; 32mo., cloth, 2s. 6d.

THOUGHTS IN PAST YEARS. 32mo., cloth, 2s. 6d.

THE SEVEN DAYS; or, The Old and New Creation. Fcap. 8vo., cloth, 3s. 6d.

THE LATE BISHOP WILBERFORCE.

SERMONS preached before the University of Oxford: Second Series, from 1847 to 1862. By the late SAMUEL WILBERFORCE, LORD BISHOP OF WINCHESTER. 8vo., cloth, 10s. 6d.
—————— Third Series, from 1863 to 1870. 8vo., cloth, 7s. 6d.
SERMONS preached on Various Occasions. With a Preface by the Lord Bishop of Ely. 8vo., cloth, 7s. 6d. [*Just published.*

REV. E. B. PUSEY, D.D.

PAROCHIAL SERMONS. Vol. I. From Advent to Whitsuntide. Seventh Edition. 8vo., cloth, 6s.
PAROCHIAL SERMONS. Vol. II. Sixth Edition. 8vo., cloth, 6s.
PAROCHIAL SERMONS. Vol. III. Reprinted from the "Plain Sermons by Contributors to the 'Tracts for the Times.'" Revised Edition, 8vo., cloth, 6s.
PAROCHIAL SERMONS preached and printed on Various Occasions. 8vo., cloth, 6s.
SERMONS preached before the University of Oxford, between A.D. 1859 and 1872. 8vo., cloth, 6s.
LENTEN SERMONS, preached chiefly to Young Men at the Universities, between A.D. 1858—1874. 8vo., cloth, 6s.
ELEVEN SHORT ADDRESSES during a Retreat of the Companions of the Love of Jesus, engaged in Perpetual Intercession for the Conversion of Sinners. 8vo., cloth, 3s. 6d.

THE LORD BISHOP OF SALISBURY.

SERMONS ON THE BEATITUDES, with others mostly preached before the University of Oxford; to which is added a Preface relating to the volume of "Essays and Reviews." New Edition. Crown 8vo., cloth, 7s. 6d.

REV. J. KEBLE.

SERMONS FOR THE CHRISTIAN YEAR. By the Rev. JOHN KEBLE, Author of "The Christian Year."
 FOR ADVENT TO CHRISTMAS EVE (46). 8vo., cloth, 6s.
 FOR CHRISTMAS AND EPIPHANY (48). 8vo., cloth, 6s.
 SERMONS FOR SEPTUAGESIMA TO LENT. 1 vol., *in preparation.*
 FOR LENT TO PASSIONTIDE (46). 8vo., cloth, 6s.
 FOR HOLY WEEK (57). 8vo., cloth, 6s.
 FOR EASTER TO ASCENSION-DAY (48). 8vo., cloth, 6s.
 FOR ASCENSION-DAY TO TRINITY SUNDAY (41). 8vo., cl., 6s.
 SERMONS FOR THE TRINITY SEASON. Two or more Volumes, 8vo., cloth, 6s. each.
 SERMONS FOR SAINTS' DAYS, (48). 8vo., *in preparation.* cloth, 6s.
 VILLAGE SERMONS ON THE BAPTISMAL SERVICE. 8vo., cloth, 5s.
 SERMONS, OCCASIONAL AND PAROCHIAL. 8vo., cloth, 12s.

JAMES PARKER AND CO.

The City of the Lost, and XIX. other Short Allegorical Sermons.

By WALTER A. GRAY, M.A. (Π.), Vicar of Arksey;—and B. KERR PEARSE, M.A. (Φ.), Rector of Ascot Heath. Fourth Edition. Fcap., cloth, 2s. 6d. *Cheap Edition*, sewed, 1s.

Rev. E. Monro.

ILLUSTRATIONS OF FAITH. Eight Plain Sermons. Fcap. 8vo., cloth, 2s. 6d.

Plain Sermons on the Book of Common Prayer. Fcap. 8vo., cloth, 5s.

Historical and Practical Sermons on the Sufferings and Resurrection of our Lord. 2 vols., Fcap. 8vo., cloth, 10s.

Sermons on New Testament Characters. Fcap. 8vo., 4s.

Lenten Sermons at Oxford.

Re-issue of the Series of Sermons preached at St. Mary's, &c.

The Series for 1857. 8vo., cloth, 5s.
For 1858. 8vo., cloth, 5s.
For 1859. 8vo., cloth, 5s.
For 1863. 8vo., cloth, 5s.
For 1866. 8vo., cloth, 5s.
For 1867. 8vo., cloth, 5s.
For 1868. 8vo., cloth, 5s.
For 1869. 8vo., cloth, 5s.
For 1870-1. 8vo., cloth, 5s.

Short Sermons for Family Reading,

Following the Course of the Christian Seasons. By the Very Rev. J. W. BURGON, B.D., Dean of Chichester. First Series. 2 vols., Fcap. 8vo., cloth, 8s.

SECOND SERIES. 2 vols., Fcap. 8vo., cloth, 8s.

Rt. Rev. J. Armstrong, D.D.

PAROCHIAL SERMONS. By the late Lord Bishop of Grahamstown. Fifth Edition. Fcap. 8vo., cloth, 5s.

SERMONS on the Fasts and Festivals. Third Edition. Fcap. 8vo., cloth, 5s.

Sermons for the Christian Seasons.

SERMONS FOR THE CHRISTIAN SEASONS. First Series. Edited by JOHN ARMSTRONG, D.D., late Lord Bishop of Grahamstown. 4 vols., Fcap. 8vo., cloth, 10s.

——————— Second Series. Edited by the Rev. JOHN BARROW, D.D., late Principal of St. Edmund Hall, Oxford. 4 vols., Fcap. 8vo., cloth, 10s.

———

OXFORD, AND 377, STRAND, LONDON.

The Service-Book of the Church of England,

A New Edition of "the Daily Services of the United Church of England and Ireland." First issued in 1849. Crown 8vo., minion type, in roan binding, 12s.; calf limp, or calf antique, 16s.; best morocco, or limp morocco, 18s.

The new "Prayer-book (Table of Lessons) Act, 1871," has necessitated reprinting nearly the whole book, and opportunity has been taken of still further adding to the improvements.

An Introduction to the Study of Gothic Architecture.

By JOHN HENRY PARKER, C.B., M.A., F.S.A. Fifth Edition, with 189 Illustrations, and a Topographical and a Glossarial Index. Fcap. 8vo., in ornamental cloth, 5s.

An Attempt to Discriminate the Styles of Architecture in England,

FROM THE CONQUEST TO THE REFORMATION: with a Sketch of the Grecian and Roman Orders. By the late THOMAS RICKMAN, F.S.A. Seventh Edition, with considerable Additions, chiefly Historical, by JOHN HENRY PARKER, C.B., M.A., F.S.A., and numerous Illustrations. Medium 8vo.

Mediæval Brasses.

A Manual of Monumental Brasses. Comprising an Introduction to the Study of these Memorials, and a List of those remaining in the British Isles. With Two Hundred Illustrations. By the late Rev. HERBERT HAINES, M.A., of Exeter College, Oxford. 2 vols., 8vo., 12s.

Mediæval Domestic Architecture.

Domestic Architecture of the Middle Ages, with numerous Engravings from Existing Remains, and Historical Illustrations from Contemporary Manuscripts. By the late T. HUDSON TURNER, Esq. From the Norman Conquest to the Thirteenth Century; interspersed with Remarks on Domestic Manners during the same Period. 8vo., cloth, £1 1s. [*Reprint.*]

From Edward I. to Richard II. (the Edwardian Period, or the Decorated Style). By the Editor of "The Glossary of Architecture." 8vo., cloth, £1 1s. *Also,*

From Richard II. to Henry VIII. (or the Perpendicular Style). With numerous Illustrations of Existing Remains from Original Drawings. In Two Vols., 8vo., £1 10s.

The Calendar of the Prayer-book.

The Calendar of the Prayer-book illustrated. (Comprising the first portion of the "Calendar of the Anglican Church," illustrated, enlarged, and corrected.) With upwards of Two Hundred Engravings from Mediæval Works of Art. Fcap. 8vo., Sixth Thousand, ornamental cloth, 6s.

Our English Home:

Its Early History and Progress. With Notes on the Introduction of Domestic Inventions. Third Edition. Crown 8vo., 3s. 6d.

JAMES PARKER AND CO., OXFORD AND LONDON.

www.ingramcontent.com/pod-product-compliance
Lightning Source LLC
Chambersburg PA
CBHW032157160426
43197CB00008B/959